Chand's Top 50 Mutual Funds

Chand's Top 50 Mutual Funds

2002 Edition

Ranga Chand

Published in 2001 by Stoddart Publishing Co. Limited
895 Don Mills Road, 400-2 Park Centre, Toronto, Canada M3C 1W3

Stoddart Books are available for bulk purchase for sales promotions, premiums, fundraising, and seminars. For details, contact the Special Sales Department at the above address.

To order Stoddart books please contact General Distribution Services
Tel. (416) 213-1919   Fax (416) 213-1917
Email cservice@genpub.com

10 9 8 7 6 5 4 3 2 1

National Library of Canada Cataloguing in Publication Data

Chand, Ranga
Chand's top 50 mutual funds

Annual.
2002 ed.-
ISSN 1700-523X
ISBN 0-7737-6234-5 (2002 ed.)

1. Mutual funds—Canada—Periodicals. I. Title. II. Title: Top 50 mutual funds.
III. Title: Chand's top fifty mutual funds.

This book contains information and statistics that have been obtained from sources that are believed to be reliable but cannot be guaranteed as to accuracy or completeness. This book is for information only and should not be construed as investment advice or a recommendation to buy, sell, or hold any securities. The data and information used in this book were obtained principally from the fund companies, their prospectuses, and Globe HySales.

The Heavy Hitters is a registered trademark of Chand Carmichael & Company Limited.

Cover design: Bill Douglas @ The Bang
Cover Photograph: Shawn Simpson
Editorial Services: Colborne Communications
Typesetting and text design: Wordstyle Productions

Printed and bound in Canada

THE CANADA COUNCIL | LE CONSEIL DES ARTS
FOR THE ARTS | DU CANADA
SINCE 1957 | DEPUIS 1957

We acknowledge for their financial support of our
publishing program the Canada Council, the Ontario Arts
Council, and the Government of Canada through the
Book Publishing Industry Development Program (BPIDP).

To Jason

Contents

Part Two
Rating the Funds

Part Three
Canadian Equity Funds

Part Four
Foreign Equity Funds

Part Five
Fixed Income and Money Market Funds

Part Six
Growth and Income Funds

Acknowledgements

I would like to thank Nelson Doucet and Donald G. Bastian of Stoddart Publishing for their continued, generous support and for their encouragement in the preparation of this premiere edition. I am also very grateful to my editors, Greg Ioannou and Leah LeDrew, and my graphic designer, Carol J. Anderson, for their extremely helpful advice and contribution to the content of this book. Thanks also to Kim Abrahamse, Eva Blank, and Jennifer Sweetlove for proofreading.

I am particularly indebted to my wife and business partner, Sylvia Carmichael, who contributed enormously to this book, and to our son, Jason, for his ongoing computer assistance.

A special thank you to all readers who have taken the time and trouble to get in touch with me with comments and questions. As always, your feedback is very much appreciated and, as you will see from this year's book, I have acted on your suggestions.

Introduction

Since our first mutual fund guide in 1994, the investment landscape has changed dramatically. Back then, there were just over 1,000 mutual funds on the market and no objective research resources available to help investors sort out the top-performing funds from the mediocre funds. That is, until *Chand's World of Mutual Funds* came on the scene and offered investors a structured quantitative approach to selecting mutual funds with proven track records. Investor response was overwhelming and the annual guide became an instant bestseller. Over the years, the guide has changed and adapted to meet investor needs, and this year is no exception.

Today investors have access to timely and virtually unlimited mutual fund information from newspapers, magazines, and the Internet. The barrier-free availability of mutual fund data on the Internet is, without a doubt, a major breakthrough for all investors. Now investors can check and compare the current and historical performance of any fund at the click of a mouse. But, with over 4,000 mutual funds now on the market, many investors are on "information overload" and simply want to cut to the chase. Judging from the hundreds of letters and e-mails we have received, this view is overwhelmingly supported by our readers.

In response to this need, the all-new *Chand's Top 50 Mutual Funds* gives investors the opportunity to fast track their mutual fund selection process by zeroing in on only the best 50 Heavy Hitter funds— those funds with proven superior track records. The system developed to identify these Heavy Hitter funds provides a structured quantitative approach to evaluating the more than 4,000 mutual funds currently available. To qualify as a Heavy Hitter and appear in *Chand's Top 50 Mutual Funds*, a fund must have the following:

- consistent top performance
- superior risk/reward ratios
- solid management

- minimum 5-year track record

- wide availability

To make investment decisions easier, *Chand's Top 50 Mutual Funds* provides a wide variety of mutual funds to choose from. These include load and no-load equity, bond, money market, foreign, and balanced funds. From this select group of overachievers, I am certain that investors will be able to find funds for their portfolios that suit their specific investment objectives and risk tolerance.

My investment philosophy, based on years of mutual fund research, is to buy funds with proven track records, monitor their performance regularly—and that's where the Internet can play a key role—and stick to long-term financial goals regardless of the market's short-term gyrations. Just as important, investors should have realistic expectations about future investment returns. I am confident that *Chand's Top 50 Mutual Funds* will help you achieve your investment goals.

Part One
Introduction to Mutual Funds

Chapter 1
What Is a Mutual Fund?

A mutual fund is a cooperative means for people with common financial goals to pool their savings. This pool of money is managed by professional money managers who, depending on the objectives of the fund, invest in anything from Government of Canada treasury bills to shares in Canadian corporations or foreign companies worldwide. These fund objectives generally cover income, growth, safety or principal, or some combination of the three.

Who Sells Mutual Funds?

Individuals can purchase mutual fund units from banks, insurance companies, brokers, financial planners, and the mutual fund's own sales force. Funds that do not charge a commission to buy, sell, or exchange fund units are called no-load funds. Sales of these funds are largely dominated by financial institutions and handled by their salaried employees. Load funds, on the other hand, charge investors a sales commission, either at the time of purchase or on redemption, and are generally offered by mutual fund companies that have limited or no salespeople of their own. These companies must rely on independent salespeople, such as brokers and financial planners, to sell their funds. The sales commission compensates the salesperson for his or her time preparing a financial plan, selecting suitable investments, and advising on matters such as retirement or estate planning.

How Do Mutual Funds Make Money?

Depending on the type of fund, mutual funds can make money from the interest paid by bonds and money market instruments (such as treasury bills) and from dividends on stocks. They can also make money from capital gains by selling securities, such as stocks and bonds, at a higher price than the fund originally paid. When a mutual fund earns money, it distributes the earnings to its unitholders in proportion to the number of units held. In this way, unitholders with small amounts of invested money get the same return per dollar as those who invest hundreds of thousands. The money earned from a fund's investments, such as interest income from bonds, is paid to unitholders as income distributions; profits from selling investments at an increased price, such as gains earned on stocks, are paid out as capital gains distributions. Investors can also make a capital gain or loss when selling back their units to the fund, depending on whether the unit price has increased or decreased since the units were originally purchased.

Of course, mutual fund companies don't provide their services for free. They charge an annual fee to cover operating expenses and management fees, which is shown as a percentage of the average net assets of the fund. Depending on the type of fund, the average management expense ratio (MER) can range anywhere from around 1% for a money market fund to about 5% for a labour sponsored venture capital fund. All other things being equal, the impact of MERs should not be overlooked, as higher expense ratios mean lower returns.

How Safe Are They?

Investing in a mutual fund is not the same as investing in a 5-year GIC. The unit price of most funds will fluctuate, some quite dramatically, and there is no guaranteed rate of return.

Because mutual funds are "securities"—not "deposits," such as chequing and savings accounts—they are not insured by the Canada Deposit Insurance Corporation (CDIC). However, unitholders' invested funds are held in trust by a custodian, usually a bank, and are protected under banking and trust laws. Securities regulations also require that companies that sell mutual fund units keep clients' funds separate from their own assets. Moreover, fund managers are prohibited from using fund assets in any way other than to make investments for the unitholders' benefit.

In addition, investors are protected by the Canadian Investor Protection Fund (CIPF) against a firm's insolvency, provided that their account is held with a mutual fund distributor or securities dealer who is a member of either the Investment Dealers Association of Canada (IDA) or one of Canada's four stock exchanges. This fund currently compensates each client up to $1 million. To find out if a company is covered in the event of insolvency, call the CIPF at 416-866-8366.

Clients of companies that are not members of the above self-regulatory organizations (SROs) are protected by various funds held by security commissions across Canada. However, the maximum compensation allowed is generally lower. In Ontario, for example, the National Contingency Trust Fund can reimburse investors up to a maximum of $5,000. Both the CIPF and the National Contingency Trust Fund are designed to reimburse individuals in the event that their mutual fund company collapses or their money is stolen in transit, but not against market losses.

Chapter 2
Advantages of Mutual Funds

Time, money, and expertise are required in varying amounts in order to build a successful investment portfolio. However, if you're fortunate enough to have large amounts of investment money at your disposal, it doesn't really matter about the other two requirements: you can hire your own money manager. For the rest of us, mutual funds level the playing field. Investing in mutual funds allows individuals with limited money, time, or investment know-how to own shares in a variety of domestic and foreign securities, all managed by a professional money manager.

For most investors, the key factors for choosing mutual funds are diversification, professional management, liquidity, ease of investment, and low cost.

Diversification
With only a limited amount of money available for investment, building a well-diversified portfolio is extremely difficult. At best, you may hold two or three stocks and possibly a bond or two. If one investment fails to perform as expected, as in the case of Bre-X or more recently Nortel, the results can be decidedly unpleasant and could seriously derail any investment plan. But, by investing the same amount of money in mutual funds, you can obtain instant diversification through funds that own bonds or shares in many different companies and countries. Bond funds typically hold around 50 to 300 issues, while equity funds might hold shares in anywhere from 20 to 100 or more companies. This spreading around of your money greatly reduces risk—if one company or one country's economy does badly, the others may do well—and increases the potential for growth of any investment portfolio. As an individual investor, you would require thousands of dollars to accomplish similar diversification.

Professional Management

Mutual funds are managed by either one person or a team. These professionals bring years of experience to the task of managing and making money. After extensive analysis of all available data, they choose which securities meet their fund's objectives and when to buy and sell. Until mutual funds came on the scene, this type of financial management was available to only large institutional investors and wealthy individuals.

Liquidity

This refers to how easily and quickly an asset, such as mutual fund units, can be converted to cash. Since mutual funds must redeem all or any of your units on demand, your assets are extremely liquid. The only exceptions are a few real estate funds, where unitholders would have to wait until the properties held were appraised. To cash in your units, all you have to do is follow the procedure given in the fund prospectus, generally a written notification. After receiving your request, the fund company will send you a cheque for the price your shares were worth on the day the company received the redemption notice. This could be greater or less than the price originally paid, depending on the market.

Ease of Investment

Buying a mutual fund is not complicated. For those with sufficient investment knowledge, a mutual fund can be bought by mail, over the phone, or on-line for those with Internet access. Those who would prefer advice in selecting an appropriate fund can take their pick from a variety of sources, such as banks, insurance companies, brokers, financial planners, and registered mutual fund specialists with individual fund companies. Most mutual fund companies also offer toll-free telephone assistance to prospective investors.

Low Cost

Because a mutual fund combines the assets it holds in trust for you with those it holds in trust for other investors, it is known as an "institutional trader" and, as such, its transaction fees to buy and sell securities are dramatically reduced. The fees a fund pays are much lower than what you would pay to buy and sell individual stocks and bonds, even from a discount broker.

Chapter 3
Types of Mutual Funds

Mutual funds buy into almost any investment vehicle you can purchase or sell on your own, such as treasury bills, bonds, stocks, real estate, and precious metals. Some funds invest only in Canada, while others search the world looking for the best investment opportunities. With well over 4,000 mutual funds on the market, it's easy to get confused. However, while no two mutual funds are exactly alike, they fall into three broad-based types: money market funds, fixed income funds, and equity funds.

Money Market Funds
The primary objective of money market funds is to preserve capital while providing income based on general interest rates. These funds invest principally in short-term (less than one year) debt securities such as federal and provincial treasury bills, guaranteed investment certificates (GICs), and bankers' acceptances (bank-guaranteed promissory notes issued by Canadian companies). In other words, the money you invest in these funds is used for short-term loans to various Canadian companies and government bodies. The aim of a money market fund is to provide investors with as high a rate of interest as possible with the lowest possible risk. Funds that invest in federal treasury bills are the safest, followed by investments in provincial treasury bills, and then investments in debentures issued by major corporations.

Unlike other mutual funds, the net asset value (NAV) of a money market fund is intended to remain fixed at $10 per unit. The NAV is the dollar value of one unit of a fund. However, investors should be aware that the rate of income may vary depending on the movement of short-term interest rates. If interest rates fall, yields may decline substantially over a short period of time.

Money market funds are suitable for investors seeking current income, a relatively secure short-term parking place, and quick and easy access to their money. They also add a conservative cushion to a diversified investment portfolio. However, over the long term, these funds provide the lowest real rate of return.

Fixed Income Funds

Bond Funds—The primary objective of bond funds, often referred to as fixed income funds, is to provide investors with a regular stream of income. These funds invest mainly in bonds and debentures issued by federal, provincial, and municipal governments and large corporations. They may also invest in company stocks that pay regular dividends. The biggest advantage of bond funds is the diversification you can get with limited amounts of money (funds typically hold from 50 to 300 issues). However, unlike bonds bought individually, bond funds do not have a fixed rate of interest or maturity date. The composition of this type of fund changes constantly due to changing markets, individual bonds in the portfolio maturing, and the manager's buying and selling decisions. Therefore, interest income payments will fluctuate. Short term bond funds (average maturities of the bonds held in the fund range from 1 to 5 years) have the least risk, followed by intermediate term bond funds (5-10 years), and then long term bond funds (over 10 years). The longer the average maturity term of the bonds held in a portfolio, the more sensitive the fund will be to interest-rate movements.

Mortgage Funds—As with bond funds, the aim of mortgage funds is to provide regular income payments. These funds generally concentrate on residential first mortgages—the most secure type—although some funds include commercial and industrial mortgages. Because fund managers rarely trade the mortgages they hold, capital-gains potential is low. Mortgage funds tend to be less volatile than most bond funds because of the shorter maturity dates of the investments held.

Fixed income funds are suitable for investors seeking a regular stream of interest income as part of a well-diversified portfolio. They are also a good choice for meeting medium-term (3-7 years) financial goals, depending on the maturity and quality of the fund's holdings. For investors who are comfortable with the added risks, which include currency exchange fluctuations, there are also foreign bond funds. These invest in debt securities of foreign governments and companies. Foreign bond funds further diversify a portfolio and provide a hedge against any decline in the value of the Canadian dollar. When the dollar falls in value against the currency of the country in which your fund holds assets, you gain. When the dollar goes up in value, however, this eats into your returns.

Equity Funds

Canadian Equity Funds—These funds, also known as "growth funds," invest in a wide range of Canadian companies through common and preferred shares, with the objective of providing long-term capital growth through increases in stock prices. Conservative equity funds typically invest in large well-established corporations with long histories of profitability. Aggressive stock funds, on the other hand, may invest in the common shares of small emerging companies, often referred to as "small-cap," that are expected to grow rapidly. The primary objective of this type of fund is to provide investors with maximum capital gains.

Although Canadian equity funds have the potential for providing higher returns over time than money market or income funds, they also carry additional risk. Because of the volatility of the stock market, and depending on the type of equity fund held, returns on these funds may vary widely from year to year. Therefore, they are not suitable for individuals with a short investment time frame.

Canadian equity funds are suitable for investors who seek long-term growth of capital, have an investment time frame of 5 years or longer, and are able to accept greater short-term fluctuations in the value of their investment. Canadian equity funds are more volatile than bond and money market funds but—because of their diversification—carry less risk than, say, investing all or most of your money in one or two stocks.

Foreign Equity Funds—These funds invest mainly in stocks of companies located around the world and are generally more volatile than their domestic counterparts. The primary objective of these funds, as with Canadian equity funds, is to provide investors with long-term capital appreciation. However, the value of foreign equity funds will be affected not only by market conditions, foreign government policies, and political uncertainties, but also by exchange-rate fluctuations (in the same way that foreign bond funds are affected). Management expenses are also higher for foreign equity funds, due to the added cost of having overseas advisors and operating in foreign markets.

Foreign equity funds are suitable for more aggressive investors who have an investment time frame of 5 years or longer, are able to accept greater short-term fluctuations in the value of their investment, and are prepared to accept the additional risks associated with investing in foreign markets. These funds are also good for adding diversification to an otherwise Canada-only portfolio and as a hedge against a decline in the value of the Canadian dollar.

Growth and Income Funds

On the domestic front, these include dividend funds and balanced and tactical asset allocation funds. These are hybrids that attempt to provide investors with long-term capital growth, combined with income.

Dividend Funds—These funds invest in dividend-paying preferred shares of Canadian corporations and in common shares that are expected to yield a high level of dividend income. As with equity funds, there is also the potential for long-term capital growth through higher share prices of the funds' holdings.

Balanced and Tactical Asset Allocation Funds—These funds are intended to provide a competitive total return through a diversified portfolio of cash, stocks, and bonds issued by federal, provincial, and municipal governments and large corporations. The objective of these types of funds is to provide investors with long-term capital growth through increases in stock prices, combined with income. Because of their diversified portfolio, these funds are less volatile than equity funds but more volatile than money market and bond funds.

Growth and income funds are suitable for investors with an investment time frame of at least 5 years, who wish to combine growth of capital and income in one fund. For investors who are comfortable with the added risks, which include currency exchange fluctuations, there are also global balanced and asset allocation funds, which invest in stocks of foreign companies and debt securities of foreign governments and companies. These funds provide added diversification to a portfolio and hedge against any decline in the value of the Canadian dollar.

Chapter 4
The Prospectus

All mutual fund companies are required to issue a prospectus—the legally required selling document—to all potential investors. Although it is not a particularly easy read, it is a must-read before investing. The document is divided into two parts: Part A provides information about the fund company and investments in general, and Part B provides specific information about each of the funds included in the prospectus. This information—in text and graphics—includes management objectives, performance, and expenses. Key points to check are listed below.

Fees and Expenses
This section lists and explains the fees and expenses, commonly known as management expense ratios (MERs), that investors pay indirectly when they invest in any of the funds included in the prospectus. Also included are the sales charges (if any) payable by the investor when buying, selling, or transferring (switching) fund units. Fund companies that charge fees to purchase their mutual funds generally offer investors the choice between buying units through either a front-end sales charge or a deferred sales charge. Front-end sales charges, also called front-end loads, are sales commissions paid at the time of purchase. Although most companies recommend a maximum sales commission between 5% and 6% of the initial dollar amount invested, the charge is generally negotiable between the investor and his or her salesperson. For investors who choose the deferred sales charge option, also known as back-end loads, fees are levied when units are sold back to the fund during the first few years after purchase. Typically, these non-negotiable charges start at 6% for redemptions during the first year of purchase and decrease to 0% after 6 or 7 years.

Investment Objectives and Strategies
Included in this section is an explanation of the fund's goals, such as seeking current income or growth of capital. It also describes the securities it

will hold in order to achieve these objectives, such as bonds or stocks. A general guideline may also be given as to what proportion the securities will represent in the fund's portfolio or which sectors the fund will emphasize, such as financial services or technology. This section will also provide information on the fund's use of derivatives or other investment strategies.

Investment Risks

This section alerts investors to the type of risk the fund is subject to, such as interest-rate, stock-market, foreign-security, derivative, or foreign-currency risk. It also provides a quick checklist that investors can use to determine if the fund is suitable for their investment objectives, time horizon, and the degree of risk they are willing to accept.

Past Performance

This section contains a chart showing the fund's annual historical return since inception and a graph comparing the growth of a $10,000 investment in the fund with the returns of an appropriate index. It is important to note that the performance returns do not take into account any sales fees or income taxes that might be payable by the investor. They also assume that all distributions made by the fund are reinvested.

Financial Highlights

This section provides a table tracking the fund's net asset value (NAV) over the most recent 5-year period. The NAV is the dollar value of one unit of a fund. Also included are the fund's MER and portfolio turnover rates over the same period.

The MER is the total of all the fees and expenses of the fund. It is calculated by dividing the fund's total expenses by its average net asset value during the year, multiplied by 100. For example, if a fund with $1 billion in assets has total yearly expenses of $20 million, its MER would be 2%. This means that out of every $100 invested, $2 goes to management fees and operating expenses. Take a good look at expense ratios. Ideally they should be decreasing over time. However, expenses of newer funds may remain high because they are still building their asset base. All posted returns for funds are net of MERs.

The fund's portfolio turnover rate reflects how frequently securities are bought and sold by the fund. A 100% turnover rate indicates that the value of the fund's holdings was completely turned over in any one year. A high turnover rate creates high brokerage costs, which means the fund needs to generate higher returns to offset these costs. Moreover, high turnover rates may increase the taxable distributions of the fund and result in tax liabilities for unitholders.

The prospectus also offers information about how to buy units in the fund, what the minimum dollar investment is, how to redeem units, and much more. The vast majority of fund companies also have toll-free numbers, should you require assistance or wish to request a copy of a fund's quarterly or annual report.

Chapter 5
Management Styles

Although the most important determinant of the performance of equity-based mutual funds is the performance of the stock market as a whole, a particular manager's investment style is not something that should be ignored. Investors are well advised to look at a manager's investment philosophy as well as a fund's past performance figures before making a buying decision. Fund managers usually adhere to one of the following approaches.

Growth

These managers look for companies with a good track record of rapid growth in sales and earnings and the potential for more of the same. Typically a growth stock will have a higher-than-average price-to-earnings ratio, and trade at a price well above book value. The belief is that the future growth of the company will, in a relatively short time frame, justify its current high price and provide even higher prices in the future. Growth investments will often be in the small-to-medium-capitalization companies.

Value

Managers who follow a value approach search for assets that are under-valued or where the manager feels the market may not be appreciating to the full potential for that company or industry. Typically these stocks sell at low price-to-earnings ratios or book value, or may have hidden assets such as real estate or trademark rights. The strategy is to buy the assets cheap and sell them when their market value rises.

Investors should also be aware that growth and value stocks tend to perform differently during the various market cycles. For example, the prices of value stocks tend to fall by less than growth stocks during down markets. On the other hand, growth stocks tend to do better in up markets.

Sector

These managers focus on specific industries, such as high technology or the financial sector, that, based on the managers' analyses, will experience the greatest growth. The investment portfolio will then be built around individual companies within these selected industries. Some sector managers attempt to forecast which areas of a market will do well in the short term. Their strategy is to get in at the bottom before others catch on.

Many managers use a blend investment style, employing a combination of growth, value, and sector strategies.

Top-Down

Managers who use a top-down approach first analyze the economy and market outlooks and then select markets and industries that they feel will outperform. These managers are more concerned with the big picture than with individual companies.

Bottom-Up

Fund managers who follow a bottom-up management style start by selecting promising individual companies, with little or no emphasis on the larger picture. Only stocks or bonds that meet these managers' investment criteria are purchased. If the managers can't find what they want, they will hold cash until they do.

Some fund managers combine top-down and bottom-up styles, determining not only the countries and industries in which to invest but also the individual companies.

Interest Rate Anticipation

When actively employed, this technique covers forecasting and analyzing the direction of the change in interest rates, the degree of the change across maturities, and the timing of the change. Any anticipated drop in interest rates would dictate an increase in the duration of the bond portfolio, and the opposite action would be called for when rates are expected to rise. That is, if a manager foresees interest rates falling in 6-months' time, for example, he or she will try to ensure the portfolio holds bonds with longer-term maturities to see the fund through the lull in interest rates; if the manager expects interest rates to go up, the shift will be made to shorter-term maturities, so that the fund can take advantage of the higher rates that will become available.

Spread Trading

This approach involves switching bond issues to take advantage of higher yields or to decrease risk without adversely affecting the yield. Spread traders analyze and closely monitor credit risk, historical yield relationships, and the yield curve. Unlike interest-rate anticipators, spread traders are very active market participants.

Although many managers remain true to one investment philosophy, others use a combination of two or more styles. None of these investment styles is better or worse, only different. Read the prospectus and annual report or call the fund company if you have any questions on a particular manager's style.

Chapter 6
Registered Retirement Savings Plans (RRSPs)

A Registered Retirement Savings Plan (RRSP) is a tax shelter, provided under the Income Tax Act, that gives individuals who file a tax return in Canada and have eligible earned income the opportunity to save money for their retirement.

The Benefits
The two main benefits of investing in an RRSP are as follows:

- Tax Reduction—The money you put into an RRSP reduces your taxable income. Depending on your tax bracket, this means that every $1,000 contributed will save you about $250 to $500 in taxes in the year you make the contribution.

- Tax-Free Compounding—All the money in an RRSP, including all distributions, is left untouched by the Canada Customs and Revenue Agency (CCRA). Let's say you invest $100 a month, compounded monthly at an 8% annual rate of return; after 30 years you will have a retirement nest egg of over $150,000. Such is the power of compounding. Taxes are paid only when you withdraw money.

Rules and Regulations
As most of us are only too aware, anything to do with the CCRA usually has lots to do with rules and regulations. RRSPs are no exception. Here are the important ones:

- The contribution limit is 18% of your previous year's earned income (earned income includes income from employment, self-employment or owning a business, rental properties, research grants, CPP disability pensions and other taxable long-term benefits, alimony and maintenance payments, royalties, and profit-sharing funds but does not include investment income, scholarships, and bursaries) minus any pension plan adjustments, to a maximum of $13,500 for 2001, plus a carry-forward of unused contribution amounts since 1991. This limit remains in place until 2003.

- The contribution deadline for 2001 is March 1, 2002.

- The foreign-content limit for the 2001 tax year is 30% of the book value of your total RRSP holdings. Amounts in excess of the limit are subject to a penalty of 1% per month.

- The maximum lifetime non-deductible overcontribution limit is $2,000. If your overcontribution is currently in excess of this amount and was made before February 27, 1995, the excess over $2,000 must be used to fund future contributions. This means that until your existing overcontribution has been reduced to $2,000, no additional RRSP contributions will be allowed.

- Cash withdrawals are subject to withholding tax at 10% for amounts up to $5,000, 20% for amounts up to $15,000, and 30% for higher amounts. Rates in Quebec are higher.

- Home Buyer's Plan (HBP) allows you to withdraw, tax-free, up to $20,000 from your RRSP to buy or build a qualifying home. The total amount withdrawn must be repaid within a period of no more than 15 years. You may also be able to participate in the HBP more than once providing you have fully repaid previous withdrawals and if certain other conditions are met.

- Further-education loans from your RRSP were made available starting in January 1999, under the Lifelong Learning Plan (LLP). You can withdraw, tax-free, up to $10,000 a year from your RRSP, to a maximum of $20,000 over 4 years, to help pay for full-time training or college or university. Repayment must start the year after you complete your program, or in the fifth year after your first withdrawal, whichever comes first. The total amount withdrawn must be repaid to your plan in equal installments over a 10-year period.

- Termination of your RRSP must occur by the end of the year you turn 69. This means that if you turn 69 years of age in 2002 you must convert your RRSP into a retirement income option by December 31, 2002. At that time, you may either withdraw your RRSP in a lump sum, transfer it to a Registered Retirement Income Fund (RRIF) or a Life Income Fund (essentially a locked-in Retirement Income Fund with annual minimum and maximum withdrawal limits), purchase an annuity, or do any combination of the above.

- To contribute the current maximum amount of $13,500, you would need to earn $75,000, before taxes, in the previous year. Confirmation of your RRSP contribution limit appears on your previous year's CCRA Notice of Assessment, or phone TIPS at 1-800-267-6999. You'll need your social insurance number, date of birth, and the income you reported on line 150 of your 2000 return.

Chapter 7
Taxes and Mutual Funds

Many people invest in mutual funds without thinking about the possible tax implications. This could be a costly oversight. Mutual fund companies "flow through" their taxable income to investors in the form of distributions. These distributions are made on a per-unit basis, so all investors receive a proportionate amount of the income earned by the fund. However, if you hold mutual funds in a tax-sheltered account, such as a Registered Retirement Savings Plan (RRSP), no taxes are payable until you start withdrawing money. That is why it's important to take full advantage of tax-deferred plans.

Income and Capital Gains Distributions

Mutual funds make two types of distributions: income distributions and capital gains distributions.

Income distributions represent all interest and dividend income earned from money market, bond, mortgage, equity, or derivative-based index funds.

Capital gains distributions represent the profit a fund makes when it sells securities such as stocks or bonds at a higher price than originally paid. If total capital gains exceed total capital losses, resulting in net realized capital gains, the difference is distributed to unitholders. Net realized capital losses are retained by the fund and used to offset capital gains.

All income and capital gains distributions from mutual funds held outside of a registered plan are subject to federal income tax. Interest income is fully taxable at your marginal tax rate (the rate payable on the last dollar you earn). For capital gains, the amount subject to tax was reduced to 50% for gains incurred on or after October 18, 2000. For capital gains incurred before that date, the amount was 66.7%, and prior to February 28, 2000, the amount was 75%.

Capital Gains and Losses

Unitholders can generate capital gains by selling units in a fund or switching from one fund to another, at a profit. Capital gains are taxable income and must be reported on your annual tax return. If you sell any units for less than what you originally paid, you incur a capital loss. Although capital losses from a security held outside a tax-deferred plan cannot be deducted from ordinary income, 50%—the allowable capital loss—can be used to reduce any taxable capital gains you made on or after October 18, 2000. For losses incurred before that date, the amount was 66.7%, and prior to February 28, 2000, the amount was 75%.

If you don't have any taxable capital gains, you can apply your allowable capital losses to any taxable capital gain realized in the previous three years, or you can carry the losses forward to be applied against any future taxable capital gains. Capital losses generated from securities held inside a tax-deferred plan cannot be used to offset taxable capital gains. To find out if you made a gain or loss when you sell or exchange fund units, you must know the original price you paid for the units and the price you received when you sold them.

Depending on how your mutual fund is set up, at tax time you will receive either a T3 Supplementary slip (for mutual fund trusts) or a T5 Supplementary slip (for mutual fund corporations). Quebec residents receive a Releve 16 slip. One slip is issued for each individual account, regardless of the number of funds held. The slip shows the total capital gains, dividends, foreign income, and interest income. This information should be transferred to the appropriate section of your income tax return, with the slip(s) attached. However, if your funds made no distributions during the year, no slip will be issued.

Capital Gains Exposure

Some funds, even ones with high tax-efficiency ratios, may have high unrealized capital gains. This could occur if the fund manager seldom sells a stock, particularly after a bull market. Depending on the value of assets in the fund, this may or may not be a problem. In a fund with $400 million in assets, $10 million of unrealized capital gains is a potential gains exposure of only 2.5%. But in a fund with only $40 million in assets, it's a hefty 25%. This could translate into a significant tax bill in the future—particularly for new investors, who end up pay-ing taxes on money made by earlier investors.

Tax-Efficiency

Tax-efficiency is the amount you get to keep after taxes, relative to a fund's nominal total return. Let's say your equity fund delivered 20%, but your net return (after paying taxes on the capital gains) is only 15%. That fund has a tax-efficiency ratio of 75%. Clearly, the closer a fund is to 100%, the more tax-efficient it is.

What makes one fund more tax-efficient than another? Clearly, funds that generate interest income taxed at your marginal tax rate will be less tax-efficient. However, equity funds can use different port-folio techniques to increase their tax-efficiency. These funds can off-set capital gains with realized losses or keep portfolio turnovers to a minimum (by contrast, some funds have a 100% turnover rate, which means they will have sold all of their securities in a given year). Portfolio managers can sell off some of the stocks that have been big winners and offset the tax liability by getting rid of some losers. To dis-courage market-timers from moving in and out, which may force managers to sell and thereby realize capital gains, some funds also impose redemption fees.

Before- and after-tax returns are given for all of the top 50 Heavy Hitters. This will allow you to compare a fund's pre-tax return with its after-tax return and measure one fund's after-tax performance against another's. These are important considerations if your mutual funds are held outside a tax-deferred plan such as an RRSP.

Strategies for Tax-Averse Investors

Investors can also follow some tax-averse strategies. Here are several tactics to help reduce the tax bite:

- Use a buy-and-hold investment strategy (see chapter 9).

- Seek out funds with low turnover rates and low unrealized capital gains. You can do this by checking with the mutual fund company or your financial advisor.

- Look for any mention of a fund's tax-efficiency in its prospectus.

- If you hold both registered and non-registered investment plans, make sure that your overall investment strategy is tax-efficient.

- Offset capital gains with losses.

- Check a fund's distribution dates before investing. If you buy units shortly before a distribution, you will be responsible for paying taxes on the distribution, but you will not gain added value for the units.

- Finally, a word on record keeping. It's important to retain all the statements you receive from your mutual fund company or plan administrator. These will provide you with an accurate record of all your transactions and show the unit prices of all purchases and sales. You may need to refer to these papers for income tax purposes.

Chapter 8

Building Your Investment Portfolio

With well over 4,000 mutual funds to choose from, selecting suitable funds may seem like a near impossible task. By concentrating your selection on the top 50 Heavy Hitters, however, you dramatically reduce the scope of your task. And, just as important, you also avoid the mediocre and poor performers. But before you rush out to buy your funds, there are a few important steps to follow.

How to Set Your Financial Goals

A clearly defined plan is the key to financial success. Are you saving for additional retirement income, a down payment on a first home, or a child's college education? Do you need growth—where the value of the amount invested will increase over time—or regular income payments? Do you simply want to preserve your capital? Once you have identified your financial goals, you must also determine how soon you need to achieve them.

Deciding when you will need your money is important. The sooner you need it, the less risk you will want to expose it to. If you'll need the money in a few years for a down payment on a house, putting your money into the stock market is not the way to go. The stock market can suffer substantial declines in any given year or even over several consecutive years. You would not have the time to recoup those losses. If you're saving for a retirement that's some 20 years away, however, you should definitely consider investing in stocks, since the stock market offers the best growth potential. With a long investment time frame, you won't need to worry about year-to-year market fluctuations.

Understanding the Risk Factor

When it comes to investments, risk is simply the possibility of monetary loss. Unfortunately, while there is no such thing as a risk-free investment, one basic rule applies to all investments: the smaller the risk, the smaller the potential return—the higher the risk, the higher the potential return. This risk/reward relationship should be a fundamental consideration when you are deciding which funds to buy. As an investor, you need to know how comfortable you are with market fluctuations that will have a negative effect on the dollar value of your portfolio holdings. This feeling is referred to as your "risk tolerance." The major investment risk factors are the following:

- Inflation Risk—This is the chance that, due to a substantial decline in the purchasing power of money, the dollar you get upon redemption of an investment will buy less than the dollar you originally invested. As you can see from the following table, even a 3% rate of inflation can cut the value of a dollar in half in 25 years.

Average Annual Rate of Inflation

YEARS	2%	3%	4%	5%
0	$1.00	1.00	1.00	1.00
5	$0.90	$0.86	$0.82	$0.78
15	$0.74	$0.64	$0.55	$0.48
25	$0.60	$0.48	$0.38	$0.30

- Interest-Rate Risk—This is the possibility that a fixed debt instrument, such as a bond, will decline in value due to a rise in interest rates. The longer the maturity of the bond, the more its price will rise and fall, depending on interest-rate movements. For example, investors in a bond fund with an average maturity of 6 years should expect, roughly, a 6% increase in returns for every 1% decline in interest rates. Conversely, if interest rates increase by 1%, returns could decline by as much as 6%. Rising interest rates can also affect stocks by making it more difficult for companies to grow and increase their profits. Rising rates also encourage investors to take money out of the stock market and put it into bonds.

- Market Risk—This is the danger that a particular stock or sector or the overall stock market will fall and the unit price, or value, of your investment will decrease. Many factors can cause stock-market fluctuations: changes in a country's economic outlook, consumer confidence, the financial health of a company, and market rumours, to name a few. Fund managers may try to deal with an overall stock-market decline by moving a larger percentage of their portfolios into cash.

You should aim to select funds that meet your investment goals and have risk levels you are comfortable with. The following table offers some general guidelines for the three basic mutual fund categories.

FUND YOUR BASIC CATEGORY	POTENTIAL OBJECTIVE	GENERALLY RISK	INVESTS IN
Money Market	Safety of Principal	Low	Treasury Bills and Short-Term Securities
Fixed Income	Regular Income	Low to High	Mortgages and Short-, Medium-, and Long-Term Bonds
Equity	Growth of Capital	Moderate to Very High	Domestic and Foreign Stocks

Reducing Risk through Asset Allocation

Now that you have defined your financial goals and have a basic understanding of risk, you can turn your attention to asset allocation. It sounds complicated but asset allocation is simply a term used to describe your division of money among a variety of domestic and international investments. This diversification is perhaps the most important rule you can follow as an investor.

The reason for diversifying is quite simple. If you spread your money among stocks, bonds, and cash, at home and abroad, the performance of your overall portfolio should be less volatile. Losses from some investments may be offset by gains in others, exposing you to less risk than if you put all your money into, say, Canadian stocks. (It also improves your chances of having investments in a market that suddenly takes off.) At the same time, proper diversification can earn you higher overall returns than you would get if you invested in only the safest, most conservative mutual funds. It is estimated that the percentage of investments that you allocate to the different asset classes accounts for more than 80% of your portfolio's return over the long term. High-worth investors may also find it a good idea to diversify among mutual fund companies. However, if you are just beginning to invest, or have less than $15,000, a balanced fund will give you good diversification through a mix of stocks, bonds, and cash—all in one fund. The following quiz will help you determine which asset allocation is suitable for you. Your total point score will steer you to an appropriate portfolio.

Investment Profile Quiz

What are your financial goals?

I am most concerned about retaining the value of my investments but would like to keep ahead of inflation.	❏	(0 points)
My goal is regular income payments with some growth potential.	❏	(5 points)
I want maximum long-term growth.	❏	(10 points)

When will you need your money?

Money intended as an emergency cash fund or for short-term goals should be held in savings accounts, money market/T-bill mutual funds, or redeemable GICs.

Under 5 years	❏	(0 points)
5 to 10 years	❏	(5 points)
10 or more years	❏	(10 points)

What's your risk tolerance?

I do not want any drop in value, even if temporary, for most of my investments.	❏	(0 points)
I could live with moderate declines of between 10% and 20% in anticipation of potentially higher long-term returns.	❏	(5 points)
Declines of 20% or more in the short-term value of my investments would not cause me concern.	❏	(10 points)

Sample Portfolios

The following investment portfolios are intended only as guides, and if you are uncomfortable with any allocation you should move to a lower-risk strategy. Seeking the help of a qualified financial advisor who will take the time to understand your own unique set of circumstances including investment goals, age, net worth, tax implications, and return expectations is also recommended.

LEGEND

Cash or
Cash Equivalent   **Income**   **Growth**
Savings accounts   GICs   Canadian equity funds
Redeemable GICs   Bond funds   Foreign equity funds
T-bill mutual funds   Mortgage funds   Sector funds
Money market funds

Portfolio I—Preservation of Capital
0–10 Points

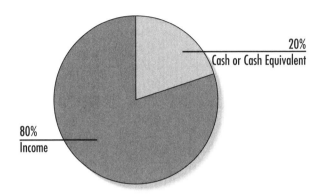

This portfolio reflects the needs of investors who want to guarantee the security of their principal and the interest income received. The income component could be split 60% in GICs staggered over various time periods and 20% in suitable bond or mortgage mutual funds. This combination of assets is best suited to investors with no- to low-risk profiles and those pursuing short-term goals. Investors who wish to add a growth option should consider 50% in GICs, 20% in fixed income mutual funds, and 10% in a Canadian equity mutual fund that invests in blue-chip companies.

Portfolio II — Income and Growth
15–20 Points

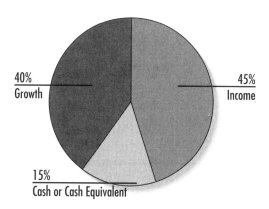

40%
Growth

45%
Income

15%
Cash or Cash Equivalent

The combination of equity and bond investments in this portfolio reduces volatility but has the potential, over time, to earn returns that will exceed inflation. Options for the income component are 15% in GICs, 15% in a bond fund, and 15% in a dividend fund. Options for the growth component are 30% in a broadly based Canadian equity mutual fund and 10% in an international equity fund. Investors who wish more growth potential could increase the equity component to 45% and reduce the income option to 40%. Individuals with more investment dollars could diversify the growth component further by including around 5% in a U.S., European, or Asia/Pacific Rim equity mutual fund.

Portfolio III—Growth
25+ Points

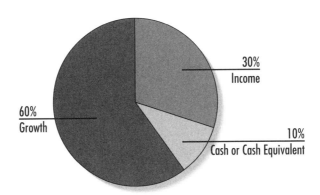

While this portfolio will display volatility from time to time, it also has the potential to provide attractive long-term growth. However, when used for shorter-term goals (under 5 years), the risk factor will significantly increase. The income component in this portfolio could be allocated as 10% in GICs, 10% a in Canadian bond fund, 5% in a dividend fund, and 5% in a foreign bond fund. Options for the growth component are 30% in a conservative Canadian equity fund, 10% in a Canadian small-cap equity mutual fund, and 20% in an international equity fund. More aggressive investors could increase the growth option to 75% or 80% by adding 5% to a fund that invests in a particular region—such as Asia/Pacific Rim or Europe—and by adding an additional 10% to a U.S. equity fund. Success with this investment strategy requires a longer investment time frame (10 or more years) and the ability to resist overreacting to market setbacks.

Selecting Your Top 50 Heavy Hitter Funds

Now that you have a good understanding of which assets and how much of each asset should be included in your investment portfolio, it's time to choose suitable Heavy Hitter funds. First, turn to the appropriate chapter, such as chapter 15 on Canadian large-cap equity funds. Here you will find important information on each fund, allowing you to easily compare the merits of investing in one fund as opposed to another.

This information includes the fund's investment style and objective, assets, some of its top 10 holdings, its best and worst returns over various time periods and the percentage of times the fund has lost money. It also includes the fund's consistency record, its risk/reward ranking, and its tax-efficiency ratio. Also shown is how a $10,000 investment would have fared over the past 5-year period, both before and after taxes. This will help you determine whether your investment should be held inside or outside a tax-deferred plan. And don't forget to check a fund's latest returns before investing. You can do this by simply calling the toll-free number given; or if you have computer access, by visiting the fund's web site (if available).

Buying Your Funds

Now that you have selected suitable funds for your investment portfolio, the next step is to buy them. The following are some of the options available.

Fund Companies. Most fund companies offer investors a family of funds that include money market, bond, and stock funds. By calling the company's toll-free number, you can request an application to open an account, and then buy and sell fund units as well as switch units from one fund to another within their family of funds. One of the advantages of dealing with only one fund company is that it eases the burden of record keeping: many companies summarize all transactions in one statement regardless of the number of funds held.

Discount Brokers. If your fund selection includes funds from different fund companies, you may want to consolidate these investments by using the services of a discount broker. Instead of filling out an application form for each fund company you wish to invest with, you complete just one application for the discount broker. With one phone call you can then buy units in a fund from one mutual fund company and sell units in a fund from a different company. The major advantage of dealing with a discount broker is the convenience of having only one point of contact for all your investment transactions. A transaction fee is charged for the services provided.

Financial Planners. If you need help restructuring your finances or with a specific issue, such as retirement planning or taxes, you may want to consult a financial planner. Common credentials for financial planners include CFP (Chartered Financial Planner), MBA (Masters in Business Administration), and RFP (Registered Financial Planner). Some financial planners charge an hourly fee while others provide their services, such as preparing a detailed financial plan, free if you buy your investments through them. Money managers usually base their fee as a percentage (typically 1%) of the assets they manage.

On-line Brokerages. On-line trading is another option for investors with Internet access. Companies such as Schwab, E*TRADE, and major discount brokerages all offer a wide selection of mutual funds on-line combined with low fees, research tools, and knowledge centers.

Do You Need a Financial Advisor?

No one can predict the future—and that includes financial advisors. So don't make the mistake of hiring one in the belief that he or she has some special insight into which markets will do well and which won't. Having said that, here are four good reasons why you might want to consider hiring a financial planner:

- You're too busy to take care of your investments yourself.

- You feel uncomfortable making investment decisions on your own.

- You need someone to help you set financial goals, prepare a financial plan, and put together an investment portfolio.

- You want advice on specific issues, such as saving for a child's education or estate planning.

Chapter 9
Different Ways of Investing

All investors use an investment strategy, even though many are unaware of it. If you bought units in a fund a number of years ago and still hold them today, you're employing a "buy-and-hold" strategy. If you automatically reinvest any fund distributions, you're already using the principle of "dollar cost averaging." However, rushing to cash in your units as soon as you see a decline in your returns is not "market timing."

Market Timing

Investors who pursue a market-timing strategy try to move in and out of stocks and bonds, hoping to invest when prices are low and sell when they are high—thereby avoiding any market declines. The difficulty with this approach is that market rallies occur in short spurts. On top of that, you have to call it right not just once, but twice. You have to know not only when to get out of the market but also when to get back in. More often than not, market-timers are "out of the market" when prices rise and there is little time for them to invest and benefit from the rally. The risk of being out of the market is very high. Numerous studies confirm this, and one by the University of Michigan, which analyzed 1,276 trading days, concluded that the cost to investors of being out of the market for just 10 days was almost one-third of the market's return.

Pros:	Trying to beat the market is fun.
Cons:	It's very difficult to do with any degree of success and on a consistent basis. Active trading increases costs and taxes and requires a lot of attention.
Best advice:	If you must play, use only a small percent of your portfolio.

Dollar Cost Averaging

This is simply investing the same amount of money at regular intervals, usually monthly or quarterly. It gets its name from "averaging out the dollar cost" of the securities you buy. This approach eliminates emotion-driven investment decisions, such as selling during a market decline (i.e., panic) and investing a lump sum during a market high (i.e., greed). Investors who contribute on a regular basis can cushion the effects of a market decline on their overall portfolio by continuing to buy when prices are near or at the bottom. When the market takes off, these purchases will show a profit. Of course, during periods when prices are higher, you'll get fewer units for your money. Most banks and mutual fund companies offer pre-authorized investment plans starting at $25. The money is withdrawn automatically from your bank account on a regular basis and invested in your selected fund(s).

Pros:	This approach takes advantage of market declines and eliminates emotion-driven investment decisions. It is ideal for individuals with small amounts to invest or those who find it hard to "pay themselves first." This is also a good way to ease large dollar amounts into the markets.
Cons:	Some investors may find this approach too rigid. It could also involve more work at tax time for investments held outside a registered plan.
Best advice:	Commit yourself to a pre-authorized monthly plan and increase the dollar amount whenever possible.

Buy and Hold

Probably the most popular strategy with mutual fund investors, this technique involves buying funds and holding on to them. The premise is that as time goes by, most of the funds will increase in value. The problem with following a strict buy-and-hold approach is the tendency for riskier funds (such as equities) to produce higher returns than more conservative funds (such as bonds). Over many years, a conservative portfolio could mutate into a somewhat risky one—not a pleasant prospect for a risk-averse investor. As well, some funds, even those with excellent track records, do nose-dive. Investors may find themselves unknowingly holding on to a fund that consistently underperforms its peers. Over time, this could have a significant drag on the overall portfolio return.

Pros: Buy and hold keeps capital gains to a minimum and requires little attention.

Cons: Poor fund performance could remain undetected. As well, the overall portfolio risk level could increase substantially over time.

Best advice: Monitor your fund's returns on a monthly or quarterly basis and rebalance assets to your original target mix at least once a year. Also, add a dash of dollar cost averaging.

While many investors stick to one investment strategy, some use a combination of two or more techniques. Regardless of what investment strategy—or combination—you use, you must first clearly define your investment objectives and how much risk you are willing to take to achieve them—this will determine your asset allocation; second, ensure that you are investing in suitable funds of well-established companies with proven track records; and third, monitor the performance of your chosen funds on a regular basis. Overlooking any one of these steps could seriously jeopardize even the most sophisticated investment strategy. (For more on monitoring, see chapter 10.)

Chapter 10

Keeping Track of Your Fund's Performance

If you invest in mutual funds, you should be prepared to spend some time monitoring their performance. As investors, we must accept that every fund, including the top 50, will have periods of underperformance from time to time.

Regular Checkups

It's a good habit to review the performance of your funds on a regular basis throughout the year. The business section of most newspapers or web sites such as *globefund.com* and *morningstar.ca* will allow you to compare your fund's return against the average for its category. Make a note of these figures, along with the date, in your investment file. Over time, any prolonged periods of underperformance—when your fund delivers below-average returns over, for example, a 12- to 18-month period—will clearly stand out. If the downward trend continues, this record will help you make more informed investment decisions, such as whether to put any new money into the fund or to redeem some or all of your units.

Why Funds Underperform

At some point, every fund manager is going to make a bad call due to sector selection, overweighting/underweighting a particular sector, or timing. For example, a manager may overweight a sector that performs poorly or underweight one that takes off. The more extreme a position the fund manager takes, the more significantly the fund's performance will be affected. Some managers may also be fully invested during market declines, with no cash to cushion the fall. Other managers may incorrectly anticipate a market decline and hold a substantial cash position, only to find the market continues its winning streak.

Rebalancing Your Portfolio

Because investments have variable rates of growth, you may have to rebalance the asset mix within your portfolio. Depending on where we are in the economic cycle, some investments will do better than others. For instance, a robust economy will boost stock prices, while a corresponding rise in interest rates will mean a drop in bond prices. Over time these events can skew your mix of investments away from your original asset allocation. This could result in a portfolio with a lot more risk that you had planned or, conversely, one with less risk and a corresponding lower return potential. To rebalance back to your original asset allocation, you can take your profits from the investments that have performed well and buy more of the asset class that has underperformed. In other words, sell high and buy low. Another option is to put any new money into the investment that has done poorly. You should review and, if necessary, rebalance your portfolio about once a year or whenever your objectives or personal circumstances change.

When to Sell a Fund

In order to make this tough decision a little easier, here are four situations in which selling a fund may make sense:

- a fund lags behind its peers over an extended period (see "Regular Checkups" above)

- the fund's objectives change and are no longer compatible with yours

- you have reached your investment goals

- your investment goals change

But remember, any selling decision should be made in combination with factors like tax implications and, in the case of funds bought under the deferred sales charge option, possible redemption penalties.

Your Investment Portfolio Return

It's extremely important to ensure that your overall investment portfolio, whether it be any number of mutual funds or a combination of different investments, is delivering the required return. For example, if your retirement plan or children's college fund is based on a 10%

average annual rate of return, you need to know that you are indeed achieving that rate of return. If you are, you can rest easy knowing your future plans are secure. If you're not, you can take steps to correct the situation such as reviewing your asset allocation (you may need to increase the growth component) or increasing your contributions. However, if, like the vast majority of investors, you simply don't bother to find out, you may discover that you have to delay your retirement or rethink the college plans.

Web Sites

For readers with Internet access, the following web sites contain a wealth of information:

- *www.fundlibrary.com* (The Fund Library)

- *www.globefund.com* (The Globe and Mail)

- *www.ific.ca* (The Investment Funds Institute of Canada)

- *www.investorlearning.ca* (Investor Learning Centre of Canada)

- *www.morningstar.ca* (Morningstar Canada)

And, of course, most of the mutual fund companies have their own web sites which offer investors a wide variety of resources.

Part Two
Rating the Funds

Chapter 11

Selecting the Top 50 Heavy Hitter Funds

With well over 4,000 mutual funds to choose from, it is no wonder that most individual investors find the process of deciding which funds to purchase not only confusing but also extremely time consuming. Many investors often consider solely short-term performance, some choose inappropriate fund categories for their investment objectives, and others simply give up and go with the hot fund of the month. Whichever tactic is used, the decision arrived at is unsatisfactory at best and dangerous at worst. *Chand's Top 50 Mutual Funds* allows investors to cut to the chase and select only the very best funds for their portfolios.

The Selection Process

In this chapter we discuss the methodology developed to identify the top 50 Heavy Hitters—those funds with a proven superior track record. To make the grade and appear in *Chand's Top 50 Mutual Funds*, a fund must have the following:

- minimum 5-year performance history

- consistent above-average returns over the past 5-year period

- outperformance of respective peer group at least 70% of the time

- superior risk/reward ratios

- consistency of investment style and sound management

- wide availability

Screening the Top 50 Heavy Hitter Funds

Performance History. With literally thousands of funds to analyze, determining the top 50 Heavy Hitters is no small task. The first basic selection criterion a fund must meet is at least a 5-year performance history. A fund with a 5-year track record gives you relevant information about how the fund has performed during the ups and downs of the economic cycle, the volatility of the fund's returns, and whether the risks of investing in it are worth the reward.

The Filtering Process. As a first step in our analysis, a fund must have posted an above-average compound return within its category over the past 5-year period. Secondly, a fund must also outperform its respective peer group on an annual basis at least 70% of the time. Here we look at a time frame from a minimum of 5 years to a maximum of 10 years. This combined focus on compound and annual performance data over an extended time period filters out funds that have, for example, performed well in only one or two years but have underperformed the rest of the time.

As a third step in becoming one of the top 50 Heavy Hitters, a fund must rank either in the first or second quintile in terms of its risk/reward ratio. As investors, we are all interested in the question of risk. How volatile are the returns of our fund? How does our fund's degree of risk compare with that of funds in the same category? Is the risk worth the reward?

To arrive at a fund's category risk/reward ranking we compare its 5-year Sharpe ratio with that of other funds in the same investment category. The Sharpe ratio is a measure of the risk-adjusted return of an investment and was developed by Nobel Prize winner William Sharpe (the ratio is calculated by dividing the rate of return for a portfolio that is above the risk-free rate, or T-Bill rate, by the standard deviation of the returns). Funds are then classified into one of five groups or quintiles—each quintile representing 20%—ranging from a high of A to a low of E. The higher the ranking, the better a fund's returns have been relative to the amount of investment risk it has taken. Only funds with a risk/reward ranking of A (top 20%) or B (top 40%) are eligible for consideration.

Management. To ensure consistency in the day-to-day decision making, the manager or lead manager must have been with the fund for at least 5 years. Certain funds have also been included in cases where the fund management style and philosophy have remained unchanged despite changes in portfolio managers.

Availability. As a final criterion, the top 50 Heavy Hitter funds must be widely available to all investors across the country, so only those funds with no restrictions are included.

Chapter 12
The Top 50 Heavy Hitter Funds at a Glance

Using our research methodology, we have identified the top 50 Heavy Hitter mutual funds in Canada. These top performers collectively manage $74 billion in assets and include 11 Canadian equity funds, 12 foreign equity funds, 15 fixed income funds, and 12 growth and income funds. Twenty-two are no-load funds and 28 are load funds. Among the Heavy Hitters, the Templeton Growth Fund—a global equity fund—is the largest, with close to $10 billion in assets. At the other end of the spectrum, the GGOF Guardian RSP Foreign Income Fund—a foreign fund—is the smallest, with $5 million in assets.

A number of fund companies have multiple Heavy Hitters. Included in this select group are Franklin Templeton, with six, and Philips Hager & North, with four. Five companies—CI Funds, HSBC, Mackenzie, Scotia, and Talvest Funds—each have three Heavy Hitters.

The chapters in parts 3, 4, 5, and 6 contain extensive information on all the top 50 Heavy Hitter funds, including assets, investment objective and style, the fund's manager, portfolio holdings, consistency record, risk/reward ranking, and tax-efficiency ratio. In addition, the fund's best and worst rolling returns for 3-month and 1-, 3-, and 5-year periods are listed. To help investors gauge the degree of risk of a particular fund, the number of times the fund lost money over each of these periods is also given.

For comparative purposes, the growth of a $10,000 initial investment over 5 years, both before and after taxes, is provided for each fund. Also included are expense ratios, minimum initial investment requirements for both RRSP and non-RRSP accounts, and the fund company's telephone number and web site (if available).

Top 50 Heavy Hitter Funds

CANADIAN EQUITY FUNDS
Canadian Equity Funds

Fund Name	Fund Family
AIC Advantage	AIC Group of Funds
AIC Diversified Canada	AIC Group of Funds
Bissett Canadian Equity	Franklin Templeton Investments
Mackenzie Ivy Canadian	Mackenzie Financial Corporation
Northwest Growth	Northwest Mutual Funds

Canadian Large-Cap Equity Funds

Fund Name	Fund Family
BMO Equity	BMO Mutual Funds
Spectrum Canadian Equity	Spectrum Investments

Canadian Small-to-Mid-Cap Equity Funds

Fund Name	Fund Family
Beutel Goodman Small Cap	Beutel Goodman Managed Funds
Fidelity Canadian Growth Company	Fidelity Investments Canada
Talvest Millennium Next Generation	Talvest Mutual Funds
Talvest Small-Cap Canadian Equity	Talvest Mutual Funds

FOREIGN EQUITY FUNDS
Global Equity Funds

Fund Name	Fund Family
AGF International Value	AGF Group of Funds
Bissett Multinational Growth	Franklin Templeton Investments
CI Global	CI Mutual Funds
Scudder Global	Scudder Group of Funds
Templeton Growth Fund	Franklin Templeton Investments
Trimark Fund	AIM Funds Management Inc.

International Equity Funds

Fund Name	Fund Family
Mawer World Investment	Mawer Mutual Funds
Templeton International Stock	Franklin Templeton Investments

U.S. Equity Funds

Fund Name	Fund Family
Investors U.S. Large Cap Value	Investors Group
McLean Budden American Equity	McLean Budden Limited

European Equity Funds

Fund Name	Fund Family
HSBC European	HSBC Investment Funds Canada
Scudder Greater Europe	Scudder Group of Funds

FIXED-INCOME FUNDS
Canadian Bond Funds

Fund Name	Fund Family
Beutel Goodman Income	Beutel Goodman Managed Funds
Bissett Bond	Franklin Templeton Investments
CI Canadian Bond	CI Mutual Funds
McLean Budden Fixed Income	McLean Budden Limited
Perigee Index Plus Bond	Perigee Mutual Funds
PH&N Bond	Phillips, Hager & North Investment Management
Scotia Canadian Income	Scotia Mutual Funds
TD Canadian Bond	TD Mutual Funds

Canadian Short-Term Bond Funds

Fund Name	Fund Family
PH&N Short Term Bond & Mortgage	Phillips, Hager & North Investment Management
Talvest Income	Talvest Mutual Fund

Canadian Mortgage Funds

Fund Name	Fund Family
HSBC Mortgage	HSBC Investment Funds Canada

Canadian Money-Market Funds

Fund Name	Fund Family
Elliott & Page Money	Elliott & Page Mutual Funds
Mackenzie Cash Management	Mackenzie Financial Corporation

Foreign Bond Funds

Fund Name	Fund Family
GGOF Guardian RSP Foreign Income	GGOF Guardian Group of Funds
Scotia CanAm US$ Income	Scotia Mutual Funds

GROWTH & INCOME FUNDS
Canadian Balanced Funds

Fund Name	Fund Family
Bissett Retirement	Franklin Templeton Investments
Mackenzie Ivy Growth & Income	Mackenzie Financial Corporation
PH&N Balanced	Phillips, Hager & North Investment Management

Canadian Tactical Asset Allocation Funds

Fund Name	Fund Family
Fidelity Canadian Asset Allocation	Fidelity Investments Canada
Mawer Canadian Diversified Investment	Mawer Mutual Funds

Canadian Dividend Funds

Fund Name	Fund Family
BMO Dividend	BMO Mutual Funds
HSBC Dividend Income	HSBC Investment Funds Canada
PH&N Dividend Income	Phillips, Hager & North Investment Management
Royal Dividend	Royal Mutual Funds
Scotia Canadian Dividend	Scotia Mutual Funds
Standard Life Canadian Dividend	Standard Life Mutual Funds

Global Balanced & Asset Allocation Funds

Fund Name	Fund Family
CI International Balanced	CI Mutual Funds

Chapter 13
A Key to the
Top 50 Heavy Hitter Tables

The following terms and statistics are used in the mutual fund pages in parts 3, 4, 5, and 6. The explanations are given in the order in which the information and data appear.

Heavy Hitter Page

Fund Name: This is the name under which the fund is currently sold.

Fund Family, Telephone Number, and Internet Address: The name of the fund family, telephone number, and Internet address (if available) are listed for ease of reference.

Fund Inception Date: This is the date the fund was launched and made available to the public. As part of the criteria to be classified as a Heavy Hitter and to be included in *Chand's Top 50 Mutual Funds*, a fund must have a performance history of at least 5 years.

Manager: The name of the portfolio manager or managers, the year they started, and their academic and/or prior investment experience are included. As part of the criteria to be identified as a Heavy Hitter, the manager(s) or lead manager must have been with the fund for at least 5 years. This ensures consistency of investment style. Certain funds have been included in cases where the management style and philosophy have remained unchanged despite changes in the portfolio managers.

Investment Objective: This is the objective of the fund, such as "aggressive growth" or "a high level of interest income," a description of the types of investments held, and any special emphasis employed by the fund manager. The investment objectives are taken directly from the fund's prospectus. For more detailed information on the different investment categories used in *Chand's Top 50 Mutual Funds*, see chapter 3 ("Types of Mutual Funds") and the specific chapters listed in parts 3, 4, 5, and 6 (e.g. chapter 14 for "Canadian Equity Funds").

Assets: The total dollar amount invested in the fund is provided.

Investment Strategy and Bias: This indicates the investment style and strategy, as well as any bias in the investment approach used by the fund (for more information on management styles, see chapter 5). The possible choices in this section include:

- Investment Style: top-down, bottom-up

- Investment Strategy: growth, value, blend

- Investment Bias: large-cap, mid-cap, small-cap

"Cap," or capitalization, is the total market value of a company and is determined by multiplying the current price of one share by the number of shares outstanding (sold). For example, a company with 10 million shares trading at $10 each would have a market capitalization of $100 million and would be considered a small company.

Portfolio: This provides the percentages invested in different market sectors, countries, and geographical areas of the world and also lists some of the top 10 holdings of the fund.

Fund Facts Page

Performance: A fund's best, worst, and average rolling returns are highlighted for 3-month and 1-, 3-, and 5-year periods.

"Rolling returns" give potential investors an additional analysis of the risk associated with investing in a fund over different time periods and different market cycles, including bull and bear markets. Rolling returns evaluate the posted rates of return of a mutual fund by analyzing the rate of return for a specified time period from a particular start date and then analyzing the rate of return for the same time frame from a start date 1-month forward. This "rollover" analysis is repeated until the fund's performance history, up to a maximum of 10 years, has been examined.

For example, let's consider a fund launched on June 1, 1990. A 3-month rolling return would evaluate the rate of return posted for the 3-month period from June 1, 1990, to August 31, 1990; then the evaluation would "roll" forward one month to consider the rate of return posted for the 3-month period from July 1, 1990, to September 30, 1990; and then from August 1, 1990, to October 31, 1990, and so on, until all possible combinations of the fund's posted rates of return have been evaluated. Similarly, a 1-year rolling return starting on the same date, June 1, 1990, would cover the 12 months to May 31, 1991; then from July 1, 1990, to June 30, 1991; and then from August 1, 1990, to July 31, 1991, and so on. The 3- and 5-year rolling returns would cover 36-month and 60-month periods, respectively.

The best 1-year rolling return, therefore, indicates the highest return over a 1-year period. Conversely, the worst 1-year rolling return indicates the lowest 1-year return during the fund's performance history, up to a maximum of 10 years.

Times Fund Lost Money (%): This indicates how often the fund lost money under the rolling returns analysis for 3-month and 1-, 3-, and 5-year periods, expressed as a percentage. For example, if an analysis of all 1-year periods shows that fund lost money 20% of the time, this means there is a 1-in-5 chance of losing money over any 1-year period. An analysis of all 3-year periods may show the same fund has lost money 5% of the time. This would indicate a decrease in risk to a 1-in-20 chance of losing money over any 3-year period.

Growth of $10,000: This chart shows the before-tax and after-tax amounts accumulated based on an initial investment of $10,000 over the 5-year period to June 30, 2001. After-tax returns assume a marginal tax rate of 50% for interest income distributions and 37.5% on capital gains distributions.

Consistency Record: This shows how often, in percentage terms, a fund has outperformed its peer group on a calendar-year basis, up to a maximum of 10 years.

Risk/Reward Ranking: As investors we are all interested in the question of risk: are the risks of investing in a particular fund delivering the reward? Only funds with superior risk/reward rankings of either an A (top 20%) or B (top 40%) are included in *Chand's Top 50 Mutual Funds* (for more on risk/reward see chapter 11).

Tax-Efficiency Ratio: This shows how much an investor gets to keep after taxes, relative to a fund's nominal total return. The closer a fund is to 100% the more tax-efficient it is (for more on tax-efficiency see chapter 7).

Fund Details: This gives the fund's management expense ratio, minimum initial investment amounts for RRSP and non-RRSP accounts, and whether or not sales charges apply.

Part Three
Canadian Equity Funds

Introduction

Canadian equity funds invest primarily in stocks of Canadian companies, with the objective of providing long-term capital growth through increases in stock prices. The funds range from all-encompassing funds that target all sectors of the economy to concentrated funds that focus on only one sector. The more conservative stock funds typically invest in large well-established corporations with long histories of profitability. Aggressive growth funds, on the other hand, may invest in the common shares of small emerging companies, often referred to as "small-cap," that are expected to grow rapidly. The primary objective of this type of fund is to provide investors with maximum capital gains.

Although all equity fund managers share the same common objective—capital appreciation—their approaches vary. Growth managers look for companies with a good track record of accelerated growth in sales and earnings and the potential for more of the same. Managers who favour a value approach search for assets that are undervalued or where the manager feels the market may not be appreciating the full potential for that company or industry. Value managers typically seek out companies with hidden assets, such as real estate or trademark rights. Some managers follow a blend approach by holding both growth and value stocks in their portfolio. Investors should also be aware that growth and value stocks tend to perform differently during the various market cycles. For example, the prices of value stocks tend to fall by less than the prices of growth stocks during bear markets. On the other hand, growth stocks tend to do better in up markets.

While equity funds have more potential for providing higher returns over time than money market or fixed income funds, they also carry additional risk. Because of the volatility of the stock market and depending on the type of equity fund held, returns on these funds may vary widely from year to year. They are, therefore, not suitable for individuals with a short investment time frame. They are also not appropriate for investors seeking current income.

Canadian equity funds are suitable for investors who have an investment time frame of at least 5 years and are able to accept greater short-term fluctuations in the value of their investment. Based on your goals and risk tolerance, you can choose from a number of Canadian equity fund categories. First-time equity investors or more cautious individuals who want the potential for long-term growth but also want to manage the risk involved may wish to consider a balanced fund, which invests in a combination of stocks and bonds (see chapter 27).

The top Heavy Hitter funds listed here cover a wide variety of investment styles—including growth, value, and a combination of growth and value. From among this group of overachievers, investors will be able to find funds for their portfolio that suit their specific investment objectives and risk tolerance.

Chapter 14
Canadian Equity Funds

Canadian equity funds invest mainly in the common shares and other equity securities of Canadian companies listed on the TSE 300 Composite Index, with the primary objective of providing long-term capital growth through increases in stock prices. Funds in this category must hold a minimum of 50% of their total assets and 75% of their non-cash assets in Canadian equities and may, at certain times, also invest in short-term debt instruments and non-Canadian securities in limited amounts for diversification.

Canadian equity funds are primarily suitable for individuals who seek long-term capital growth, have an investment time frame of at least 5 years, and are comfortable with the short-term fluctuations in the value of their investment. They are not suitable for investors with short investment time horizons or those who have a low risk tolerance. They are also unsuitable for investors seeking current income.

Of the over 440 Canadian equity funds, only five—or 1%—met the criteria to be included in *Chand's Top 50 Mutual Funds*.

AIC Advantage Fund
Family: AIC Group of Funds
Tel: 800-263-2144
Web site: www.aicfunds.com

The AIC Advantage Fund was launched in September 1985 and has been managed by Michael Lee-Chin since its inception. Lee-Chin is a graduate of McMaster University with a degree in civil engineering and is the chief executive officer of AIC Limited. When Lee-Chin acquired the company in 1987 it had little more than $1 million in assets. Today, with its strategy of investing in only a concentrated number of businesses and its particular focus on the wealth management industry, the company now manages over $14 billion in assets.

The investment objective of this load fund is to provide long-term growth of capital through investments primarily in Canadian companies, with an emphasis on the financial services sector. With an eye on the future, Lee-Chin has concentrated the fund's investments into sectors such as health care, wealth management, and information, which he believes will grow at above-average rates fuelled in part by the demographics of the baby boomers.

With over $2.5 billion in assets, the fund follows an investment strategy that is a blend of value and growth and currently has a large-cap equity bias. The fund holds less than 20 securities in its portfolio and is heavily weighted in the financial services, communications, and merchandising sectors, which account for over 55% of the fund's assets. The fund's top 10 holdings make up over 80% of the portfolio and include names such as the Toronto-Dominion Bank, Loblaws, Berkshire Hathaway, AGF Management, and CI Funds.

The AIC Advantage Fund has a high risk/reward ranking and a superior consistency record, having beaten its peer group for 8 of the past 10 years. Although there is a 1-in-20 chance that returns will be negative over any 3-year period, the fund has made money for its investors over all 5-year periods. Looking at all 5-year rolling periods, returns have averaged 19.4%, ranging from a high of 39.4% to a low of 2.2%. Given Lee-Chin's classic buy-and-hold investment strategy, this fund is also an excellent choice for investors who are looking for a tax-efficient Canadian equity fund for their non-registered plans.

Fund Facts

Fund:	AIC ADVANTAGE
Manager:	Michael Lee-Chin
Category:	Canadian Equity

Best/Worst Rolling Returns

3-Month Period

Best: 28.9%
Worst: -25.1%
Average: 5.4%
Times fund lost money: 31%

1-Year Period

Best: 94.3%
Worst: -19.4%
Average: 24.4%
Times fund lost money: 25%

3-Year Period

Best: 53.7%
Worst: -2.9%
Average: 23.5%
Times fund lost money: 5%

5-Year Period

Best: 39.4%
Worst: 2.2%
Average: 19.4%
Times fund lost money: 0%

Performance Record

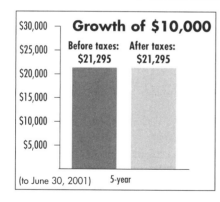

Growth of $10,000

Before taxes: $21,295 After taxes: $21,295

(to June 30, 2001) 5-year

Consistency Record 80%

Risk/Reward Ranking A

Tax-Efficiency Ratio 100%

Fund Details

Mgmt. Expense Ratio	2.45%	Sales charges	Yes
Minimum RRSP	$250	Minimum non-RRSP	$250

See chapter 13 for a discussion on how to interpret the Fund Facts page.

AIC Diversified Canada Fund

Family: AIC Group of Funds
Tel: 800-263-2144
Web site: www.aicfunds.com

The AIC Diversified Canada Fund was launched in December 1994 and has been managed by Jonathan Wellum since its inception. Wellum, a CFA with an MBA from McMaster University, heads up Georgian Capital Partners Inc., the sub-advisors to the fund. Wellum is a bottom-up stock picker who zeroes in on cash flow, management skills, and the market dominance of a company.

The objective of this load fund is to provide long-term growth of capital by investing in the common shares of Canadian and U.S. companies across a broad range of industries. Wellum focusses on the financial services and media sectors, specifically wealth management and protection, retail, investment banking, and businesses with world-class distribution and content.

With over $3.8 billion in assets, the fund follows an investment strategy that is a blend of value and growth and currently has a large-cap equity bias. The fund holds about 25 securities in its portfolio and is heavily weighted in the financial services, industrial products, media, and consumer staples sectors, which account for over 75% of the fund's assets. The fund's top 10 holdings make up about 65% of the portfolio and include names such as Bombardier, the Toronto-Dominion Bank, DuPont Canada, and the American International Group.

Wellum follows a buy-and-hold investment strategy, making this another excellent choice for investors seeking a tax-efficient equity fund. The AIC Diversified Canada Fund also has a superior risk/reward and consistency record. During the 2000/2001 bear market the fund posted a return of 0.2%, outperforming the average Canadian equity fund (largely due to its lack of exposure to Nortel and its underweighting in technology), which posted a return of -11.8%. Although there is a 1-in-4 chance that returns will be negative over a 3-month period and a 1-in-6 chance they will be negative over a 1-year period, the fund has made money for its investors over all 3- and 5-year periods. Looking at all 5-year rolling periods, returns have averaged 23.4%, ranging from a high of 27.3% to a low of 18.7%.

Fund Facts

Fund:	AIC DIVERSIFIED CANADA
Manager:	Jonathan Wellum
Category:	Canadian Equity

Best/Worst Rolling Returns

3-Month Period

Best: 24.8%
Worst: -18.9%
Average: 5.7%
Times fund lost money: 28%

1-Year Period

Best: 76.4%
Worst: -13.0%
Average: 26.3%
Times fund lost money: 18%

3-Year Period

Best: 45.9%
Worst: 2.1%
Average: 21.1%
Times fund lost money: 0%

5-Year Period

Best: 27.3%
Worst: 18.7%
Average: 23.4%
Times fund lost money: 0%

Performance Record

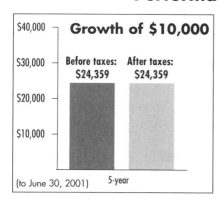

$40,000
$30,000
$20,000
$10,000

Growth of $10,000

Before taxes: $24,359   After taxes: $24,359

(to June 30, 2001)   5-year

Consistency Record 83%

Risk/Reward Ranking A

Tax-Efficiency Ratio 100%

Fund Details

Mgmt. Expense Ratio	2.45%	Sales charges	Yes
Minimum RRSP	$250	Minimum non-RRSP	$250

See chapter 13 for a discussion on how to interpret the Fund Facts page.

Bissett Canadian Equity Fund
Family: Franklin Templeton Investments
Tel: 800-387-0830
Web site: www.franklintempleton.ca

The Bissett Canadian Equity Fund was launched in February 1983 and has been managed by Fred Pynn since 1987. A chartered accountant with a CFA, Pynn has been in the investment business for over 14 years. He is a vice-president of equities and is a member of the firm's investment committee. Bissett & Associates of Calgary merged with Franklin Templeton Investments in the Fall of 2000.

This fund, originally sold through the F Series as a no-load, is now only available to new investors through the Advisor Series. The objective of this load fund is to provide long-term capital growth through a diversified portfolio of common shares of Canadian companies. Pynn is a bottom-up stock picker who follows Bissett's proven investment style, which is best described as "Growth at a Reasonable Price." Pynn and his investment team focus on revenue and earnings growth, cash flows, a company's ability to finance future growth internally, and future-growth potential.

With over $860 million in assets, the fund follows a growth investment strategy and has a mid- to large-cap equity bias. The fund holds over 150 securities in its portfolio and has positions in all the major market segments. It has significant weightings in the financial services, industrial products, and oil and gas sectors, which together account for over 50% of its assets. The fund's top 10 holdings make up about 30% of the portfolio and include Magna International, CAE Inc., and Canadian National.

A consistent performer, the fund also has a very high tax-efficiency ratio of 99% over 5 years. Although there is a 1-in-4 and a 1-in-8 chance returns will be negative over a 3-month and 1-year period respectively, the fund has made money over all 3- and 5-year periods. Looking at all 5-year rolling periods, returns have averaged 17.8%, ranging from a high of 23.9% to a low of 12.7%. The fund has posted positive returns for 9 of the past 10 calendar years, with returns ranging from a high of 36% in 1996 to a low of –2.3% in 1994.

Fund Facts

Fund:	BISSETT CANADIAN EQUITY
Manager:	Fred E. Pynn
Category:	Canadian Equity

Best/Worst Rolling Returns

3-Month Period

Best: 20.8%
Worst: -23.4%
Average: 3.8%
Times fund lost money: 27%

1-Year Period

Best: 55.4%
Worst: -15.0%
Average: 16.9%
Times fund lost money: 13%

3-Year Period

Best: 31.4%
Worst: 3.3%
Average: 15.9%
Times fund lost money: 0%

5-Year Period

Best: 23.9%
Worst: 12.7%
Average: 17.8%
Times fund lost money: 0%

Performance Record

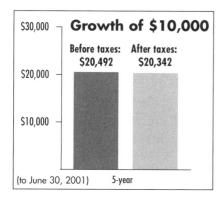

Growth of $10,000

Before taxes: $20,492   After taxes: $20,342

(to June 30, 2001)   5-year

Consistency Record   80%

Risk/Reward Ranking   A

Tax-Efficiency Ratio   99%

Fund Details

Mgmt. Expense Ratio	1.27%	Sales charges	Yes
Minimum RRSP	$500	Minimum non-RRSP	$500

See chapter 13 for a discussion on how to interpret the Fund Facts page.

Mackenzie Ivy Canadian Fund

Family: Mackenzie Financial Corporation

Tel: 800-387-0614
Web site: www.mackenziefinancial.com

The Mackenzie Ivy Canadian Fund was launched in October 1992 and is co-managed by the team of Jerry Javasky and Chuck Roth. Together they have over 30 years of combined investment management experience. Javasky, a chartered accountant with an MBA from York University has been with the fund since May 1997, and Roth, a CFA, joined in 1999. Javasky and Roth are also the co-managers of the Mackenzie Ivy Growth and Income Fund, another top 50 Heavy Hitter fund.

The objective of this load fund is to seek capital appreciation by primarily investing in a select group of high-quality Canadian businesses. The fund typically invests in large-cap companies that the managers believe will deliver above-average returns combined with lower-than-average risk levels. The managers follow a disciplined approach focussing on a company's competitive and financial position, management strength, and expected profitability. The fund usually holds less than 75 securities and may invest up to 30% in foreign equities.

With over $5 billion in assets, the fund follows a value investment style. It currently holds about 35 securities in its portfolio with 66% of its assets invested in Canada, another 20% in the U.S., and about 11% in cash. It has significant weightings in the financial, industrial, consumer, communications, and energy sectors, which together account for over 85% of its assets. The fund's top 10 holdings make up about 40% of the portfolio and include well-known companies such as George Weston Ltd., the Royal Bank of Canada, Berkshire Hathaway, and Petro-Canada.

The Mackenzie Ivy Canadian Fund has an excellent risk/reward ranking as well as a superior tax-efficiency ratio of 95% over 5 years. During the 2000/2001 bear market this fund posted a return of 0.7%, outperforming the average Canadian equity fund, which posted a return of −11.8%. Although there is a 1-in-5 and a 1-in-11 chance returns will be negative over a 3-month and 1-year period respectively, the fund has made money over all 3- and 5-year periods. Looking at all 5-year rolling periods, returns have averaged 13.4%, ranging from a high of 16.0% to a low of 11.5%.

Fund Facts

Fund:	MACKENZIE IVY CANADIAN
Manager:	Jerry Javasky and Chuck Roth
Category:	Canadian Equity

Best/Worst Rolling Returns

3-Month Period

Best: 14.2%
Worst: -13.6%
Average: 2.9%
Times fund lost money: 19%

1-Year Period

Best: 31.8%
Worst: -3.7%
Average: 12.6%
Times fund lost money: 9%

3-Year Period

Best: 20.3%
Worst: 5.3%
Average: 12.9%
Times fund lost money: 0%

5-Year Period

Best: 16.0%
Worst: 11.5%
Average: 13.4%
Times fund lost money: 0%

Performance Record

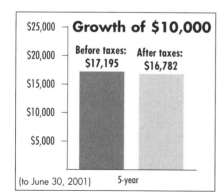

Growth of $10,000

Before taxes: $17,195
After taxes: $16,782

(to June 30, 2001) 5-year

Consistency Record 75%

Risk/Reward Ranking A

Tax-Efficiency Ratio 95%

Fund Details

Mgmt. Expense Ratio	2.47%	Sales charges	Yes
Minimum RRSP	$500	Minimum non-RRSP	$500

See chapter 13 for a discussion on how to interpret the Fund Facts page.

Northwest Growth Fund

Family: Northwest Mutual Funds

Tel: 888-809-3333
Web site: www.northwestfunds.com

The Northwest Growth Fund was launched in February 1992 and has been managed by Richard Fogler since 1995. Fogler, a graduate of the Wharton School at the University of Pennsylvania who also pursued post-graduate studies at the Sorbonne in France, has over 25 years of investment experience. He is managing director and chief investment officer of the investment firm Kingwest and Company, the managers of the fund.

The investment objective of this load fund is to provide long-term capital growth through investment primarily in stocks of Canadian companies. In making his stock picks, Fogler uses the "Economic Value Added" principle of only selecting companies that are creating shareholder value. Companies are only considered if they have demonstrated an ability to generate superior cash return on invested capital and dominate an industry due to a strong competitive advantage. In addition, Fogler looks for companies whose management thinks and acts like a shareholder.

With over $140 million in assets, the fund follows a bottom-up value investment style and can invest in small-, medium-, and large-cap equities. It currently holds about 40 securities in its portfolio with 60% of its assets invested in Canada, another 20% in the U.S., and just over 15% in cash. It has significant weightings in the financial services, industrial products, and oil and gas sectors, which together account for over 40% of its assets. The fund's top 10 holdings make up about 40% of the portfolio and include Kingsway Financial Services, Shaw Communications, the Royal Bank of Canada, and AT&T.

The Northwest Growth Fund has an excellent risk/reward ranking. During the 2000/2001 bear market the fund posted a return of 5.0%, outperforming the average Canadian equity fund, which posted a return of –11.8%. Although there is a 1-in-4 chance that returns will be negative over a 3-month period and a 1-in-6 chance they will be negative over a 1-year period, the fund has made money for its investors over all 3- and 5-year periods. Looking at all 5-year rolling periods, returns have averaged 13.1%, ranging from a high of 16.7% to a low of 7.2%.

Fund Facts

Fund:	NORTHWEST GROWTH
Manager:	Richard L. Fogler
Category:	Canadian Equity

Best/Worst Rolling Returns

3-Month Period

Best: 18.2%
Worst: -20.9%
Average: 3.2%
Times fund lost money: 26%

1-Year Period

Best: 36.4%
Worst: -19.1%
Average: 13.7%
Times fund lost money: 16%

3-Year Period

Best: 20.3%
Worst: 5.1%
Average: 12.3%
Times fund lost money: 0%

5-Year Period

Best: 16.7%
Worst: 7.2%
Average: 13.1%
Times fund lost money: 0%

Performance Record

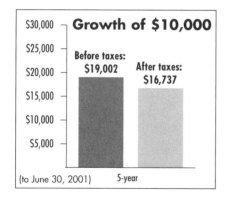

Growth of $10,000

Before taxes: $19,002
After taxes: $16,737

(to June 30, 2001)   5-year

Consistency Record	75%
Risk/Reward Ranking	A
Tax-Efficiency Ratio	79%

Fund Details

Mgmt. Expense Ratio	3.05%	Sales charges	Yes
Minimum RRSP	$500	Minimum non-RRSP	$500

See chapter 13 for a discussion on how to interpret the Fund Facts page.

Chapter 15
Canadian Large-Cap Equity Funds

The investment objective of Canadian large-cap equity funds is to provide long-term capital growth through increases in stock prices. To achieve this objective, these funds typically invest in large well-established Canadian companies listed on the TSE 100 Index that have long histories of profitability and whose stocks provide the best capital-appreciation potential. Many Canadian large-cap equity fund portfolios include such well-known names as BCE Inc., the Royal Bank, and Bombardier.

Canadian large-cap equity funds are suitable for individuals who seek long-term capital growth, have an investment time frame of at least 5 years, and are comfortable with the short-term fluctuations in the value of their investment. Canadian large-cap equity funds are not suitable for investors with short investment time horizons, those who have a low risk tolerance, or those seeking current income.

Of the 140 Canadian large-cap equity funds, only two met the criteria to be included in *Chand's Top 50 Mutual Funds*.

BMO Equity Fund

Family: BMO Mutual Funds
Tel: 800-665-7700
Web site: www.bmo.com

The BMO Equity Fund was launched in May 1993 and has been managed by Michael Stanley since its inception. Stanley, the head of Canadian equity management at Jones Heward Investment Counsel, is a CFA with an MBA from the University of Toronto, and has been in the investment business for more than 20 years. Jones Heward, a subsidiary of the Bank of Montreal, is the advisor to the fund. Stanley is also the manager of the BMO Dividend Fund, another top 50 Heavy Hitter fund.

The investment objective of this no-load fund is to seek long-term capital growth by investing in well-established Canadian businesses. Stanley, a bottom-up stock picker, focusses on factors such as the company's price/book value, potential for growth, and senior management's quality of leadership. He also carefully monitors the companies that he invests in for any changes that may affect their profitability.

With over $1.4 billion in assets, the fund follows an investment style that is a blend of growth and value with a large-cap equity bias. The fund is well diversified and holds about 150 securities in its portfolio. It has positions in all the major market segments with significant weightings in the financial services, industrial products, and the oil and gas sectors, which together account for about 55% of assets. The fund's top 10 holdings make up about 35% of the portfolio and include the Royal Bank of Canada, CIBC, the Bank of Nova Scotia, Bombardier, and Suncor Energy.

Ranking in the top 25% of its category over the past 5 years, the BMO Equity Fund has an excellent risk/reward ranking as well as a superior tax-efficiency ratio of 92%. Although there is a 1-in-4 chance that returns will be negative over a 3-month period and a 1-in-4 chance they will be negative over a 1-year period, the fund has made money for its investors over all 3- and 5-year periods. Looking at all 5-year rolling periods, returns have averaged 14.6%, ranging from a high of 20.2% to a low of 7.6%.

Fund Facts

Fund:	BMO EQUITY
Manager:	Michael Stanley
Category:	Canadian Large-Cap Equity

Best/Worst Rolling Returns

3-Month Period

Best: 18.9%
Worst: -23.3%
Average: 3.0%
Times fund lost money: 28%

1-Year Period

Best: 46.5%
Worst: -14.5%
Average: 14.3%
Times fund lost money: 24%

3-Year Period

Best: 23.6%
Worst: 6.1%
Average: 14.6%
Times fund lost money: 0%

5-Year Period

Best: 20.2%
Worst: 7.6%
Average: 14.6%
Times fund lost money: 0%

Performance Record

Growth of $10,000

Before taxes: $18,935
After taxes: $18,004

(to June 30, 2001)   5-year

Consistency Record   71%

Risk/Reward Ranking   A

Tax-Efficiency Ratio   92%

Fund Details

Mgmt. Expense Ratio	2.34%	Sales charges	No
Minimum RRSP	$500	Minimum non-RRSP	$500

See chapter 13 for a discussion on how to interpret the Fund Facts page.

Spectrum Canadian Equity Fund

Family: Spectrum Investments

Tel: 877-732-8786
Web site: www.spectrum.com

The Spectrum Canadian Equity Fund was launched in 1971 and has been co-managed by Brian Dawson and Susan Shuter since May 1999. With close to 30 years of combined investment experience, Dawson and Shuter, both CFAs, are portfolio managers with the investment firm McLean Budden, the manager of the fund.

The investment objective of this load fund is to achieve long-term capital growth by investing primarily in a broadly-diversified portfolio of large Canadian companies. In selecting stocks for the portfolio, the managers use a disciplined, bottom-up stock picking process to evaluate a company's current position and future prospects. They also utilize top-down risk controls to achieve broad diversification across all the major industry sectors. About 95% of the fund's portfolio is invested in stocks. About 70% is invested in Canada, 15% is invested in the United States, and just over 10% is invested internationally.

With close to $1.6 billion in assets, the fund follows an investment style that is a blend of growth and value with a large-cap equity bias. The fund is well-diversified and holds about 170 securities in its portfolio. It has positions in all the major market segments with significant weightings in the financial services, industrial products, and the oil and gas sectors, which together account for about 40% of assets. The fund's top 10 holdings make up about 30% of the portfolio and include the Royal Bank of Canada, CIBC, the Bank of Nova Scotia, Bombardier, and Alcan.

The Spectrum Canadian Equity Fund has a superior risk/reward ranking and an excellent consistency record, having beaten its peer group for 8 of the past 10 years. Although there is a 1-in-4 chance that returns will be negative over a 3-month period and a 1-in-6 chance they will be negative over a 1-year period, the fund has made money over all 3- and 5-year periods. Looking at all 5-year rolling periods, returns have averaged 14.0%, ranging from a high of 19.8% to a low of 7.1%.

Fund Facts

Fund:	SPECTRUM CANADIAN EQUITY
Manager:	Brian Dawson and Susan Shuter
Category:	Canadian Large-Cap Equity

Best/Worst Rolling Returns

3-Month Period

Best: 17.7%
Worst: -24.3%
Average: 3.3%
Times fund lost money: 26%

1-Year Period

Best: 45.4%
Worst: -20.9%
Average: 15.0%
Times fund lost money: 16%

3-Year Period

Best: 21.3%
Worst: 4.8%
Average: 13.0%
Times fund lost money: 0%

5-Year Period

Best: 19.8%
Worst: 7.1%
Average: 14.0%
Times fund lost money: 0%

Performance Record

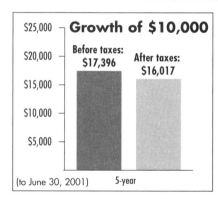

Consistency Record	80%
Risk/Reward Ranking	B
Tax-Efficiency Ratio	84%

Fund Details

Mgmt. Expense Ratio	2.57%	Sales charges	Yes
Minimum RRSP	$500	Minimum non-RRSP	$500

See chapter 13 for a discussion on how to interpret the Fund Facts page.

Chapter 16

Canadian Small-to-Mid-Cap Equity Funds

The investment objective of Canadian small-to-mid-cap equity funds is to provide maximum capital gains. To achieve this objective, these funds typically invest in IPOs and stocks of small- and medium-sized Canadian companies that have a market capitalization—the number of shares multiplied by the price per share—of less than $500 million. Because small companies start from a much smaller base, they can often grow at a much faster rate than larger companies. For example, it is much easier for a company with revenues of $20 million to double its sales, compared to a company with revenues of $20 billion. However, the short-term records of many small companies make this type of fund more speculative than other Canadian equity funds.

These funds are suitable for aggressive, long-term investors who seek the potential for high capital gains and are comfortable with the short-term, and sometimes dramatic, fluctuations in the value of their investment. This volatility makes them unsuitable for conservative investors or those with short investment time horizons. These funds are also unsuitable for investors seeking current income.

Of about 130 Canadian small-to-mid-cap equity funds, only four met the criteria to be included in *Chand's Top 50 Mutual Funds*.

Beutel Goodman Small-Cap Fund
Family: Beutel Goodman Managed Funds
Tel: 800-461-4551
Web site: www.beutel-can.com

The Beutel Goodman Small-Cap Fund was launched in January 1995 and has been managed by the company's investment management team since its inception. Beutel Goodman, which was established in 1967, is one of Canada's largest independent investment managers with close to $14 billion under management. The company, in its quest for achieving superior long-term returns, uses a value philosophy that is backed up with strong internal research.

The investment objective of this no-load fund is to seek long-term capital growth through investments in Canadian companies that the managers believe will experience the fastest growth. The fund invests in a diversified group of small company stocks whose companies typically have a market capitalization of up to $300 million.

With just over $40 million in assets, the fund follows a bottom-up value investment style. The fund holds about 40 securities in its portfolio and has significant weightings in the industrial products, consumer products, real estate, and the oil and gas sectors, which together account for about 65% of assets. The top 10 holdings make up about 45% of the portfolio and include the Mosaic Group, Moore Corporation, Brookfield Properties, Magellan Aerospace, and Athabasca Oil Sands.

The Beutel Goodman Small-Cap Fund has an excellent risk/reward ranking. During the 2000/2001 bear market this fund posted a return of 8.2%, outperforming the average Canadian small-to-mid-cap equity fund, which posted a return of –11.4%. The fund also has a very good overall consistency record, having beaten its peer group for 4 of the past 5 years. Although there is a 1-in-4 chance that returns will be negative over a 3-month period and a 1-in-7 chance they will be negative over a 1-year period, the fund has made money for its investors over all 3- and 5-year periods. Looking at all 5-year rolling periods, returns have averaged 17.6%, ranging from a high of 20.1% to a low of 13.0%. For the first half of 2001, the fund delivered a return of 16.9% compared to its peer group average of 2.3%.

Fund Facts

Fund:	BEUTEL GOODMAN SMALL-CAP
Manager:	Management team
Category:	Canadian Small-to-Mid-Cap Equity

Best/Worst Rolling Returns

3-Month Period

Best: 21.5%
Worst: -21.3%
Average: 4.8%
Times fund lost money: 25%

1-Year Period

Best: 64.3%
Worst: -16.9%
Average: 19.4%
Times fund lost money: 15%

3-Year Period

Best: 28.7%
Worst: 5.0%
Average: 13.9%
Times fund lost money: 0%

5-Year Period

Best: 20.1%
Worst: 13.0%
Average: 17.6%
Times fund lost money: 0%

Performance Record

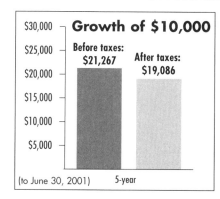

Growth of $10,000

Before taxes: $21,267
After taxes: $19,086

(to June 30, 2001) 5-year

Consistency Record 80%

Risk/Reward Ranking A

Tax-Efficiency Ratio 85%

Fund Details

Mgmt. Expense Ratio	1.46%	Sales charges	No
Minimum RRSP	$10,000	Minimum non-RRSP	$10,000

See chapter 13 for a discussion on how to interpret the Fund Facts page.

Fidelity Canadian Growth Company Fund

Family: Fidelity Investments Canada

Tel: 800-263-4077

Web site: www.fidelity.ca

The Fidelity Canadian Growth Company Fund was launched in July 1994 and has been managed by Alan Radlo since its inception. Radlo, who received his BA from Brandeis University and his MBA from the University of Massachusetts, also manages Canadian and U.S. pension accounts for Fidelity and in total manages close to $9 billion.

The investment objective of this load fund is to seek long-term capital growth by focussing primarily on small- and medium-sized companies. Radlo picks stocks using Fidelity's traditional bottom-up investment approach, which includes fundamental analysis and seeking out undervalued companies with innovative, committed management and products or services that offer the potential for accelerated earnings growth. The company's investment strategy focusses on the strengths of individual stocks rather than on market trends.

With just over $2.6 billion in assets, the fund holds about 120 securities in its portfolio and has significant weightings in the industrial products, oil and gas, and financial services sectors, which together account for just over 50% of assets. The top 10 holdings represent about 30% of the fund's assets and include Sun Life and the National Bank of Canada in the financial services sector, Canadian Hunter Exploration and Penn West Petroleum in the oil and gas sector, and C-MAC Industries in the industrial products sector.

The Fidelity Canadian Growth Company Fund has an excellent risk/reward ranking and a very good overall consistency record, having beaten its peer group for 5 of the past 6 years. Although there is a 1-in-5 chance that returns will be negative over a 3-month period and a 1-in-8 chance they will be negative over a 1-year period, the fund has made money for its investors over all 3- and 5-year periods. Looking at all 5-year rolling periods, returns have averaged 18.9%, ranging from a high of 23.7% to a low of 15.2%. The fund has posted positive returns for each of the past 6 calendar years with returns ranging from a high of 31.1% in 1995 to a low of 4.5% in 1998.

Fund Facts

Fund: FIDELITY CANADIAN GROWTH COMPANY
Manager: Alan Radlo and Maxime Lemieux
Category: Canadian Small-to-Mid-Cap Equity

Best/Worst Rolling Returns

3-Month Period

Best: 29.5%
Worst: -20.9%
Average: 4.5%
Times fund lost money: 22%

1-Year Period

Best: 42.4%
Worst: -12.1%
Average: 20.0%
Times fund lost money: 12%

3-Year Period

Best: 28.5%
Worst: 7.4%
Average: 18.4%
Times fund lost money: 0%

5-Year Period

Best: 23.7%
Worst: 15.2%
Average: 18.9%
Times fund lost money: 0%

Performance Record

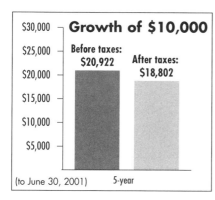

Growth of $10,000
Before taxes: $20,922
After taxes: $18,802
(to June 30, 2001) 5-year

Consistency Record 83%

Risk/Reward Ranking A

Tax-Efficiency Ratio 85%

Fund Details

Mgmt. Expense Ratio	2.52%	Sales charges	Yes
Minimum RRSP	$500	Minimum non-RRSP	$500

See chapter 13 for a discussion on how to interpret the Fund Facts page.

Talvest Millennium Next Generation Fund
Family: Talvest Mutual Funds
Tel: 800-268-0081
Web site: www.talvest.com

The Talvest Millennium Next Generation Fund was launched in December 1993 and has been managed by Leslie Williams since its inception. Williams, a chartered accountant, has been managing money for close to 30 years and is with Morrison Williams Investment Management, the advisors to the fund.

The investment objective of this load fund is to seek long-term capital growth by focussing primarily on small-to-mid-cap companies. The fund invests in a diversified portfolio of Canadian and foreign equities that Williams believes will provide the best opportunity for capital appreciation. Williams is especially bullish on the industrial products sector—particularly non-technology companies—and in the oil and gas sector, which he believes will continue to benefit from robust demand in the short-term.

With just over $91 million in assets, the fund follows a top-down investment style that is a blend of growth and value. The fund holds about 25 securities in its portfolio and has positions in virtually all the major market segments. Its heavy concentration in the industrial products and oil and gas sectors account for close to 40% of its assets. The top 10 holdings make up about 60% of the portfolio and include the Standard & Poor's 400 Mid-Cap Depository Receipts, AGF Management, PanCanadian Petroleum, and Canadian Hunter Exploration. Over 75% of its assets are invested in Canada, 15% is in the United States, and about 10% is in cash.

The Talvest Millennium Next Generation Fund has an excellent risk/reward ranking and a very good overall consistency record, having beaten its peer group for 6 of the past 7 years. Although there is a 1-in-3 chance that returns will be negative over a 3-month period and a 1-in-5 chance they will be negative over a 1-year period, the fund has made money for its investors over all 3- and 5-year periods. Looking at all 5-year rolling periods, returns have averaged 17.8%, ranging from a high of 22.6% to a low of 10.0%.

Fund Facts

Fund: TALVEST MILLENNIUM NEXT GENERATION
Manager: Leslie Williams
Category: Canadian Small-to-Mid-Cap Equity

Best/Worst Rolling Returns

3-Month Period

Best: 25.2%
Worst: -22.8%
Average: 3.9%
Times fund lost money: 34%

1-Year Period

Best: 71.1%
Worst: -27.4%
Average: 19.1%
Times fund lost money: 21%

3-Year Period

Best: 38.7%
Worst: 3.0%
Average: 17.6%
Times fund lost money: 0%

5-Year Period

Best: 22.6%
Worst: 10.0%
Average: 17.8%
Times fund lost money: 0%

Performance Record

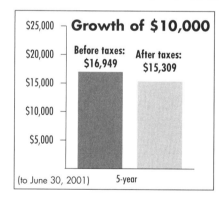

Growth of $10,000

Before taxes: $16,949
After taxes: $15,309

(to June 30, 2001) 5-year

Consistency Record 86%
Risk/Reward Ranking A
Tax-Efficiency Ratio 80%

Fund Details

Mgmt. Expense Ratio	2.50%	Sales charges	Yes
Minimum RRSP	$500	Minimum non-RRSP	$500

See chapter 13 for a discussion on how to interpret the Fund Facts page.

Talvest Small-Cap Canadian Equity Fund

Family: Talvest Mutual Funds
Tel: 800-268-0081
Web site: www.talvest.com

The Talvest Small-Cap Canadian Equity Fund was launched in November 1993 and has been managed by Sebastian Van Berkom since its inception. Van Berkom, who has specialized in small-cap investing since 1971, is the president of the Montreal investment firm Van Berkom & Associates, the advisors to the fund.

The investment objective of this load fund is superior long-term growth of capital through investments in the common shares of Canadian companies that Van Berkom believes are undervalued or have above-average growth potential. He looks for high-quality, early-established small-cap companies and tends to avoid niche players and micro-caps (new, relatively untested companies with higher risk). Van Berkom also seeks out investment opportunities in companies with new products and/or markets and companies involved in reorganizations or acquisitions.

With about $230 million in assets, the fund follows a bottom-up/growth investment style. The fund holds about 80 securities in its portfolio and has positions in virtually all the major market segments. It is heavily concentrated in the industrial products, consumer products, financial services, and oil and gas sectors, which together account for over 70% of its assets. The top 10 holdings make up about 30% of the portfolio and include Shaw Industries, the Gennum Corporation, AGF Management, Dorel Industries, and Van Houtte Ltd.

The Talvest Small-Cap Canadian Equity Fund has a very good overall consistency record, having beaten its peer group for 5 of the past 6 years. During the 2000/2001 bear market this fund posted a return of 1.1%, outperforming the average Canadian small-to-mid-cap equity fund, which posted a return of –11.4%. Although there is a 1-in-11 chance that returns will be negative over any 3-year period, the fund has made money for its investors over all 5-year periods. Looking at all 5-year rolling periods, returns have averaged 13.1%, ranging from a high of 16.1% to a low of 9.1%.

Fund Facts

Fund: TALVEST SMALL-CAP CANADIAN EQUITY
Manager: J. Sebastian Van Berkom
Category: Canadian Small-to-Mid-Cap Equity

Best/Worst Rolling Returns

3-Month Period

Best: 24.1%
Worst: -27.7%
Average: 2.8%
Times fund lost money: 36%

1-Year Period

Best: 59.3%
Worst: -30.3%
Average: 13.6%
Times fund lost money: 22%

3-Year Period

Best: 31.0%
Worst: -1.3%
Average: 13.3%
Times fund lost money: 9%

5-Year Period

Best: 16.1%
Worst: 9.1%
Average: 13.1%
Times fund lost money: 0%

Performance Record

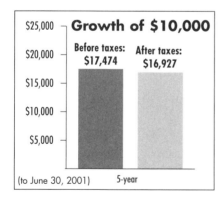

$25,000 — **Growth of $10,000**

Before taxes: **$17,474** After taxes: **$16,927**

$20,000
$15,000
$10,000
$5,000

(to June 30, 2001)   5-year

Consistency Record   83%

Risk/Reward Ranking   A

Tax-Efficiency Ratio   94%

Fund Details

Mgmt. Expense Ratio   2.70%   Sales charges   Yes
Minimum RRSP $500   Minimum non-RRSP $500

See chapter 13 for a discussion on how to interpret the Fund Facts page.

Part Four
Foreign Equity Funds

Introduction

Foreign equity funds range from broad-based global equity funds that invest in all regions of the world to country-specific funds. The primary objective of these funds, as with Canadian equity funds, is to provide investors with long-term capital appreciation through investments primarily in common stocks. However, the value of these funds will be affected not only by political uncertainties and market conditions but also by exchange-rate fluctuations. When the dollar falls in value against the currency of the country in which your fund holds assets, you gain. When the Canadian dollar rises in value, this will eat into your returns. This makes these funds generally more volatile than their domestic counterparts. Management expenses are also higher for foreign equity funds, due to the added cost of having overseas advisors and operating in foreign markets.

Since non-Canadian markets tend to move independently of the Canadian stock market, foreign equity funds provide investors with added diversification and lower the risk of the total portfolio. For example, when Canadian markets are in decline, Europe or Asia may be rising. Based on your investment objectives and risk tolerance, you can choose from a number of foreign equity fund categories, including the more broadly diversified world equity and international equity funds as well as region-specific funds such as U.S. equity and European equity.

Foreign equity funds are suitable for more aggressive investors who have an investment time frame of at least 5 years, are able to accept greater short-term fluctuations in the value of their investment, and are prepared to assume the additional risks associated with investing in international markets. These funds are also good for providing added diversification to a Canada-only portfolio and as a hedge against a decline in the value of the Canadian dollar. These funds are not suitable for cautious or conservative investors or those individuals with a short investment time horizon.

The top 50 Heavy Hitter mutual funds listed here cover a wide variety of investment styles and offer individuals the choice of investing in broadly diversified funds that hold securities in both North America and overseas or ones that invest exclusively in a specific region, such as Europe. From among this group of overachievers, investors seeking foreign exposure will be able to find funds for their portfolio that suit their specific investment objectives and risk tolerance.

Chapter 17
Global Equity Funds

Global equity funds invest primarily in a diversified portfolio of stocks of companies from around the world, including Canada, with the basic objective of achieving long-term capital growth through increases in stock prices. By diversifying investments on a worldwide basis, these funds tend to be less volatile than funds that invest in a particular country or region.

These funds are suitable for investors who seek long-term growth of capital, have an investment time horizon of at least 5 years, and are comfortable with short-term, and sometimes significant, fluctuations in the value of their investment. These funds are also good for providing added diversification to a Canada-only portfolio, and as a hedge against any decline in the value of the Canadian dollar. However, potential investors should be prepared to assume the additional risks associated with investing in international markets. These funds are not suitable for short investment time horizons, those who have a low risk tolerance, or those seeking current income.

Of the 460 global equity funds, only six met the criteria to be included in *Chand's Top 50 Mutual Funds*.

AGF International Value Fund

Family: AGF Group of Funds
Tel: 800-268-8583
Web site: www.agf.com

The AGF International Value Fund was launched in June 1989 and has been co-managed by Charles Brandes and Jeff Busby since 1994. Brandes is a recognized leader in value investing and the author of Value Investing Today. He founded Brandes Investment Partners, which is based in San Diego, California, in 1976. Busby has an MBA from the University of California, is a managing partner with the firm, and has over 20 years of investment experience.

The investment objective of this load fund is to provide long-term capital growth by investing in a diversified portfolio of common shares of global companies. Brandes and Busby follow a classic Benjamin Graham—the originator of the value investing strategy— bottom-up, value-oriented approach in their stock selection. As part of their investment strategy, the managers employ computerized screening and fundamental analysis to identify around 100 stocks from an initial database of about 10,000 companies around the world.

With over $6.6 billion in assets, the fund follows a bottom-up/value investment strategy with a large-cap equity bias. The fund holds over 70 securities in its portfolio with 55% of its assets invested in the United States, another 14% in the United Kingdom, and just over 10% in Japan. The Pacific Rim accounts for about 13% of assets and Latin America accounts for 7%. The fund's top 10 holdings make up about 30% of the portfolio and include well-known names such as Goodyear, Philip Morris, Unilever, Xerox, and Zurich Financial Services.

A consistent top-quartile performer, the AGF International Value Fund has an excellent risk/reward and consistency record. During the 2000/2001 bear market, this fund posted a return of 15.4%, outperforming the average global equity fund, which posted a return of –16.4%. Although there is a 1-in-5 chance that returns will be negative over a 3-month period and a 1-in-100 chance they will be negative over a 1-year period, the fund has made money for its investors over all 3- and 5-year periods. Looking at all 5-year rolling periods, returns have averaged 19.4%, ranging from a high of 22.2% to a low of 16.4%.

Fund Facts

Fund: AGF INTERNATIONAL VALUE
Manager: Charles Brandes and Jeff Busby
Category: Global Equity

Best/Worst Rolling Returns

3-Month Period

Best: 20.0%
Worst: -10.9%
Average: 4.7%
Times fund lost money: 22%

1-Year Period

Best: 42.9%
Worst: -0.9%
Average: 20.2%
Times fund lost money: 1%

3-Year Period

Best: 25.7%
Worst: 15.0%
Average: 19.7%
Times fund lost money: 0%

5-Year Period

Best: 22.2%
Worst: 16.4%
Average: 19.4%
Times fund lost money: 0%

Performance Record

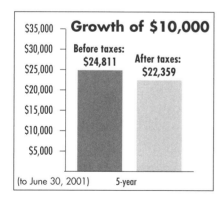

Growth of $10,000

Before taxes: $24,811
After taxes: $22,359

(to June 30, 2001) 5-year

Consistency Record 83%

Risk/Reward Ranking A

Tax-Efficiency Ratio 88%

Fund Details

Mgmt. Expense Ratio	2.80%	Sales charges	Yes
Minimum RRSP	$100	Minimum non-RRSP	$1,000

See chapter 13 for a discussion on how to interpret the Fund Facts page.

Bissett Multinational Growth Fund
Family: Franklin Templeton Investments
Tel: 800-387-0830
Web site: www.franklintempleton.ca

The Bissett Multinational Growth Fund was launched in July 1994 and has been managed by Jeffrey Morrison since February 1999. Morrison, a CFA, joined Bissett in 1998 and is a member of the investment committee. Although Morrison has been with the fund for less than 3 years, Bissett follows a disciplined team approach and each equity manager is committed to the "Growth at a Reasonable Price" investment philosophy. This ensures consistency in the management of their funds. Bissett & Associates of Calgary merged with Franklin Templeton Investments in the Fall of 2000.

This fund, originally sold through the F Series as a no-load, is now only available to new investors through the company's Advisor Series. The objective of this fund is to provide long-term capital appreciation by investing in stocks of North American and international companies that obtain a significant portion of their revenue and earnings from global operations. Morrison focusses on companies that have a record of growing earnings and dividends.

With over $140 million in assets, the fund follows a bottom-up/growth investment strategy with a large-cap equity bias. The fund holds about 45 securities in its portfolio, with 65% of its assets invested in North America, 25% in Europe, and about 5% in Asia and the Pacific Rim. The fund's top 10 holdings make up about 30% of the portfolio and include Microsoft, Exxon Mobil, JP Morgan Chase, Johnson & Johnson, IBM, and AstraZeneca.

The Bissett Multinational Growth Fund has an excellent risk/reward ranking and a very high tax-efficiency ratio of 96% over 5 years. During the 2000/2001 bear market, this fund posted a return of –0.9%, outperforming the average global equity fund, which posted a return of –16.4%. Although there is a 1-in-5 chance that returns will be negative over a 3-month period and a 1-in-33 chance they will be negative over a 1-year period, the fund has made money over all 3- and 5-year periods. Looking at all 5-year rolling periods, returns have averaged 18.9%, ranging from a high of 21.1% to a low of 15.4%.

Fund Facts

Fund:	BISSETT MULTINATIONAL GROWTH
Manager:	Jeffrey Morrison
Category:	Global Equity

Best/Worst Rolling Returns

3-Month Period

Best: 19.0%
Worst: -12.3%
Average: 4.2%
Times fund lost money: 22%

1-Year Period

Best: 52.8%
Worst: -2.9%
Average: 19.3%
Times fund lost money: 3%

3-Year Period

Best: 31.0%
Worst: 5.2%
Average: 19.9%
Times fund lost money: 0%

5-Year Period

Best: 21.1%
Worst: 15.4%
Average: 18.9%
Times fund lost money: 0%

Performance Record

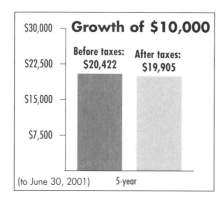

Growth of $10,000
$30,000
$22,500
$15,000
$7,500
Before taxes: $20,422
After taxes: $19,905
(to June 30, 2001)   5-year

Consistency Record 83%

Risk/Reward Ranking A

Tax-Efficiency Ratio 96%

Fund Details

Mgmt. Expense Ratio	1.45%	Sales charges	Yes
Minimum RRSP	$500	Minimum non-RRSP	$500

See chapter 13 for a discussion on how to interpret the Fund Facts page.

CI Global Fund

Family: CI Mutual Funds
Tel: 800-563-5181
Web site: www.cifunds.com

The CI Global Fund was launched in February 1986 and has been managed by William Sterling since 1990. Sterling, with a PhD from Harvard University, is chief investment officer with CI Global Advisors. With over 18 years of investment experience, he is the co-author of the best-selling book *Boomernomics*, which focussed on how to integrate demographics and investing. Sterling is also the manager of the CI International Balanced Fund, another top 50 Heavy Hitter fund.

The investment objective of this load fund is to provide maximum long-term capital growth. Sterling focusses on the stocks of established companies throughout the world that have good prospects for future growth. Sterling combines a top-down analysis of global macro-economic trends with bottom-up research, to select companies that offer the best growth potential. In other words, he not only takes into account the big picture, but also scrutinizes each investment at the company level.

With over $2.7 billion in assets, the fund follows a top-down investment strategy that is a blend of growth and value with a large-cap equity bias. The fund holds about 170 securities in its portfolio with close to 60% of its assets invested in the United States, another 12% in Japan, and around 8% in Europe. The fund also holds about 5% of its assets in emerging markets and just over 10% in cash. The fund's top 10 holdings make up about 17% of the portfolio and include Citigroup, General Electric, AT&T, Alcoa, and the Bank of New York.

The CI Global Fund has an excellent consistency record, having beaten its peer group for 8 of the past 10 years. Although there is a 1-in-3 chance that returns will be negative over a 3-month period and a 1-in-6 chance they will be negative over a 1-year period, the fund has made money over all 3- and 5-year periods. Looking at all 5-year rolling periods, returns have averaged 14.7%, ranging from a high of 23.6% to a low of 10.4%.

Fund Facts

Fund: CI GLOBAL
Manager: William Sterling
Category: Global Equity

Best/Worst Rolling Returns

3-Month Period

Best: 35.2%
Worst: -16.0%
Average: 3.3%
Times fund lost money: 29%

1-Year Period

Best: 55.7%
Worst: -24.7%
Average: 15.3%
Times fund lost money: 16%

3-Year Period

Best: 29.8%
Worst: 4.4%
Average: 14.8%
Times fund lost money: 0%

5-Year Period

Best: 23.6%
Worst: 10.4%
Average: 14.7%
Times fund lost money: 0%

Performance Record

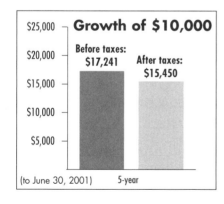

Growth of $10,000
Before taxes: $17,241
After taxes: $15,450
(to June 30, 2001) 5-year

Consistency Record	80%
Risk/Reward Ranking	B
Tax-Efficiency Ratio	79%

Fund Details

Mgmt. Expense Ratio	2.53%	Sales charges	Yes
Minimum RRSP	$500	Minimum non-RRSP	$500

See chapter 13 for a discussion on how to interpret the Fund Facts page.

Scudder Global Fund
Family: Scudder Group of Funds
Tel: 888-462-9986
Web site: www.scudder.ca

The Scudder Global Fund was launched in October 1995 and has been co-managed by the team of William Holzer and Nicholas Bratt since its inception. With close to 50 years of combined investment experience, Holzer has the day-to-day responsibility for the fund's worldwide strategy and investment themes while Bratt is responsible for Scudder's overall global equity investment strategies.

This fund, originally sold through the Classic Series as no-load, is now only available through the company's Advisor Series. The objective of this fund is to provide long-term capital growth by investing in the stocks of established companies, primarily in the industrial economies. The managers concentrate on companies that will benefit from key global and industry themes instead of focussing on specific country weightings.

With over $80 million in assets, the fund follows a bottom-up/value investment strategy with a large-cap equity bias. The fund holds about 100 securities in its portfolio with close to 40% of its assets invested in the United States, another 16% in the United Kingdom, and around 13% in Japan. The fund is well-diversified across the major market segments with significant weightings in the financial, energy, consumer, and industrial sectors, which together account for about 50% of its assets. The fund's top 10 holdings make up about 20% of the portfolio and include Burlington Resources, Conoco, Rio Tinto, the Exelon Corporation, and the Lockheed Martin Corporation.

The Scudder Global Fund has an excellent consistency record, having beaten its peer group for 4 of the past 5 years. Although there is a 1-in-3 and a 1-in-11 chance that returns will be negative over a 3-month and 1-year period respectively, the fund has made money over all 3- and 5-year periods. Looking at all 5-year rolling periods, returns have averaged 14.1%, ranging from a high of 16.5% to a low of 11.6%. The fund has posted positive returns for each of the past 5 calendar years with returns ranging from a high of 21.6% in 1999 to a low of 0.4% in 2000.

Fund Facts

Fund:	SCUDDER GLOBAL
Manager:	William Holzer and Nicholas Bratt
Category:	Global Equity

Best/Worst Rolling Returns

3-Month Period

Best: 15.2%
Worst: -8.3%
Average: 3.3%
Times fund lost money: 30%

1-Year Period

Best: 29.5%
Worst: -11.4%
Average: 15.2%
Times fund lost money: 9%

3-Year Period

Best: 21.0%
Worst: 5.2%
Average: 16.0%
Times fund lost money: 0%

5-Year Period

Best: 16.5%
Worst: 11.6%
Average: 14.1%
Times fund lost money: 0%

Performance Record

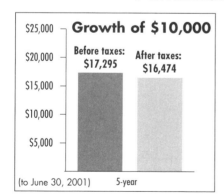

Growth of $10,000
$25,000
$20,000 — Before taxes: $17,295   After taxes: $16,474
$15,000
$10,000
$5,000
(to June 30, 2001)   5-year

Consistency Record 80%

Risk/Reward Ranking A

Tax-Efficiency Ratio 91%

Fund Details

Mgmt. Expense Ratio	2.25%	Sales charges	Yes
Minimum RRSP	$500	Minimum non-RRSP	$500

See chapter 13 for a discussion on how to interpret the Fund Facts page.

Templeton Growth Fund
Family: Franklin Templeton Investments
Tel: 800-387-0830
Web site: www.franklintempleton.ca

The Templeton Growth Fund, one of the oldest and largest funds in Canada, was launched in November 1954 and has been managed by George Morgan since the beginning of 2001. Morgan, a CFA with an MBA from the University of Western Ontario, joined Franklin Templeton in 1995 and has over 13 years of investment experience. Although Morgan has been with the fund for a short time, the firm has a strong commitment to the founder Sir John Templeton's disciplined philosophy of "value, patience, and bottom-up investing." This ensures consistency in the management of their funds.

The investment objective of this load fund is to provide long-term capital growth through investments in a diversified portfolio of common stocks of companies located around the world. The firm's strict adherence to building a portfolio stock by stock and from the bottom up ensures broad diversification by country, by region, and by industry group.

With over $9.8 billion in assets, this mega-fund follows a bottom-up/value investment strategy. The fund holds about 150 securities in its portfolio with about 40% of its assets invested in the United States, 11% in the United Kingdom, 6% each in Japan and Hong Kong, and 2% to 3% in various other countries, including the Netherlands, South Korea, Australia, and Sweden. The fund's top 10 holdings make up about 17% of the portfolio and include Cheung Kong Holdings, Albertson's Inc., Abbott Laboratories, Motorola, and Hitachi.

The Templeton Growth Fund has a good risk/reward ranking and an excellent consistency record, having beaten its peer group for 8 of the past 10 years. During the 2000/2001 bear market, this fund posted a return of 1.1% outperforming the average global equity fund, which posted a return of –16.4%. Although there is a 1-in-4 chance that returns will be negative over a 3-month period and a 1-in-16 chance they will be negative over a 1-year period, the fund has made money over all 3- and 5-year periods. Looking at all 5-year rolling periods, returns have averaged 13.7%, ranging from a high of 19.0% to a low of 8.8%.

Fund Facts

Fund: TEMPLETON GROWTH

Manager: George Morgan

Category: Global Equity

Best/Worst Rolling Returns

3-Month Period

Best: 15.7%
Worst: -15.7%
Average: 3.3%
Times fund lost money: 26%

1-Year Period

Best: 41.5%
Worst: -11.1%
Average: 13.8%
Times fund lost money: 6%

3-Year Period

Best: 23.1%
Worst: 2.9%
Average: 13.2%
Times fund lost money: 0%

5-Year Period

Best: 19.0%
Worst: 8.8%
Average: 13.7%
Times fund lost money: 0%

Performance Record

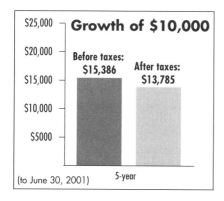

Growth of $10,000

Before taxes: $15,386
After taxes: $13,785

(to June 30, 2001) 5-year

Consistency Record 80%

Risk/Reward Ranking B

Tax-Efficiency Ratio 74%

Fund Details

Mgmt. Expense Ratio	2.21%	Sales charges	Yes
Minimum RRSP	$500	Minimum non-RRSP	$500

See chapter 13 for a discussion on how to interpret the Fund Facts page.

Trimark Fund

Family: AIM Funds Management Inc.
Tel: 800-874-6275
Web site: www.aimfunds.ca

The Trimark Fund was launched in September 1981 and is co-managed by the experienced team of Judith Adams, Bill Kanko, and Tye Bousada. Adams and Kanko, both CFAs, took over the management of this fund in 1999. Their combined 35 years of investment experience and their adherence to the fund's investment philosophy has resulted in a quartile-1 performance for the fund. Bousada, a CFA with over 7 years experience in the industry, joined the team in December 2000.

The investment objective of this front-end load fund is to provide long-term capital growth by investing in stocks of companies located anywhere around the globe. In making their stock picks, the managers place particular emphasis on those companies that have strong management, are dominant in their industry, and are expected to focus on productivity and competitiveness to improve their market share.

With over $3.1 billion in assets, the fund follows a bottom-up investment strategy with a large-cap equity bias. The fund holds a concentrated portfolio of about 40 securities. Over 60% of the fund's assets are invested in the United States, another 13% is in Japan, and close to 10% is in Europe. The fund also holds about 11% in cash. The fund's top 10 holdings make up about 35% of the portfolio and include Harrahs Entertainment Inc., Canon Inc., Moody's Corporation, FedEx, Knight Ridder, and American Express.

The Trimark Fund has an excellent risk/reward ranking. During the 2000/2001 bear market, the fund posted a return of 8.7%, outperforming the average global equity fund, which posted a return of –16.4%. Although there is a 1-in-5 chance that returns will be negative over a 3-month period and a 1-in-25 chance they will be negative over a 1-year period, the fund has made money over all 3- and 5-year periods. Looking at all 5-year rolling periods, returns have averaged 15.9%, ranging from a high of 23.6% to a low of 11.3%. The fund has posted positive returns for each of the past 10 calendar years, with returns ranging from a high of 31.6% in 1993 to a low of 6.4% in 1998.

Fund Facts

Fund: TRIMARK

Manager: Judith Adams, Bill Kanko, and Tye Bousada

Category: Global Equity

Best/Worst Rolling Returns

3-Month Period

Best: 24.2%
Worst: -15.0%
Average: 4.2%
Times fund lost money: 21%

1-Year Period

Best: 45.8%
Worst: -13.4%
Average: 17.4%
Times fund lost money: 4%

3-Year Period

Best: 27.9%
Worst: 7.3%
Average: 15.9%
Times fund lost money: 0%

5-Year Period

Best: 23.6%
Worst: 11.3%
Average: 15.9%
Times fund lost money: 0%

Performance Record

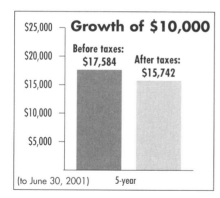

Growth of $10,000

Before taxes: $17,584
After taxes: $15,742

(to June 30, 2001)   5-year

Consistency Record 70%

Risk/Reward Ranking A

Tax-Efficiency Ratio 80%

Fund Details

| Mgmt. Expense Ratio | 1.62% | Sales charges | Yes |
| Minimum RRSP | $500 | Minimum non-RRSP | $500 |

See chapter 13 for a discussion on how to interpret the Fund Facts page.

Chapter 18
International Equity Funds

International equity funds invest primarily in a diversified portfolio of stocks of companies from around the world, excluding Canada, with the basic objective of achieving long-term capital growth through increases in stock prices. By diversifying investments on a worldwide basis, these funds tend to be less volatile than funds that invest in a particular country or region.

International equity funds are suitable for investors who seek long-term growth of capital, have an investment time frame of at least 5 years, and are comfortable with short-term, and sometimes significant, fluctuations in the value of their investment. These funds are also good for adding diversification to a Canada-only portfolio and as a hedge against any decline in the value of the Canadian dollar.

Potential investors should, however, be prepared to assume the additional risks associated with investing in international markets. International equity funds are not suitable for investors with short investment time horizons or those with a low risk tolerance. They are also unsuitable for those investors seeking current income.

Of the close to 170 international equity funds, only two met the criteria to be included in *Chand's Top 50 Mutual Funds*.

Mawer World Investment Fund

Family: Mawer Mutual Funds
Tel: 888-549-6248
Web site: www.mawer.com

The Mawer World Investment Fund was launched in November 1987 and has been managed by Gerald Cooper-Key since its inception. Cooper-Key, a CFA with more than 35 years of investment experience, is in charge of international equities at Mawer Investment Management, a privately owned investment counselling firm based in Calgary.

The investment objective of this no-load fund is to provide long-term capital growth by investing in a diversified portfolio of international equities. The fund invests in countries outside North America, including Europe, Asia, Latin America, and Australia.

Cooper-Key uses a bottom-up investment style coupled with fundamental analysis to identify many of the world's top companies that are trading at a discount to their North American counterparts. He focusses on industries that exist outside of North America and companies whose value has not yet been fully recognized by investors.

With over $85 million in assets, the fund holds over 50 securities in its portfolio. About 45% of the fund's portfolio is invested in Europe, another 24% is in the United Kingdom, and just over 10% is in Japan. The fund also has around a 20% exposure to emerging markets. The fund's top 10 holdings make up about 30% of the portfolio and include Tomra Systems, Peugeot, Barclays Bank, Telefonica SA, Nokia, and Canon Inc.

The Mawer World Investment Fund has an excellent consistency record, having beaten its peer group for 8 of the past 10 years. It also has a very good risk/reward ranking and during the 2000/2001 bear market it outperformed the average international equity fund, which posted a return of –19.2%, by 7.7%. Although there is a 1-in-4 chance that returns will be negative over a 3-month period and a 1-in-9 chance they will be negative over a 1-year period, the fund has made money over all 3- and 5-year periods. Looking at all 5-year rolling periods, returns have averaged 14.3%, ranging from a high of 19.0% to a low of 10.0%.

Fund Facts

Fund: MAWER WORLD INVESTMENT
Manager: Gerald A. Cooper-Key
Category: International Equity

Best/Worst Rolling Returns

3-Month Period

Best: 28.1%
Worst: -13.7%
Average: 3.3%
Times fund lost money: 27%

1-Year Period

Best: 42.5%
Worst: -11.7%
Average: 14.6%
Times fund lost money: 11%

3-Year Period

Best: 22.8%
Worst: 7.1%
Average: 14.2%
Times fund lost money: 0%

5-Year Period

Best: 19.0%
Worst: 10.0%
Average: 14.3%
Times fund lost money: 0%

Performance Record

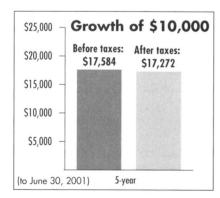

Growth of $10,000

Before taxes: $17,584
After taxes: $17,272

(to June 30, 2001) 5-year

Consistency Record 80%

Risk/Reward Ranking A

Tax-Efficiency Ratio 97%

Fund Details

Mgmt. Expense Ratio	1.56%	Sales charges	No
Minimum RRSP	$5,000	Minimum non-RRSP	$5,000

See chapter 13 for a discussion on how to interpret the Fund Facts page.

Templeton International Stock Fund

Family: Franklin Templeton Investments
Tel: 800-387-0830
Web site: www.franklintempleton.ca

The Templeton International Stock Fund was launched in January 1989 and has been managed by Don Reed since its inception. Reed is president and chief executive officer of Templeton Management Ltd. and is responsible for managing both global and international portfolios. Amongst his many activities, Reed also co-founded the International Society of Financial Analysts and serves on the Women in Capital Markets Advisory Board—an organization based in Toronto that promotes the entry, development, and advancement of women in the capital markets.

The objective of this load fund is to achieve long-term capital growth by investing in the securities of companies or governments located outside the U.S. and Canada. Reed follows the classic Templeton philosophy of bottom-up/value investing, choosing solid companies whose stock is trading at prices that are undervalued in relation to their intrinsic value and potential.

With over $6.0 billion in assets, the fund is the largest international equity fund in Canada. The fund holds close to 90 securities in its portfolio with close to 65% of the fund's assets invested in Europe, about 25% in Asia and the Pacific Rim, and less than 5% in Latin America. The top 10 holdings make up just over 20% of the portfolio and include Unilever, Pechiney, Deutsche Post, East Japan Railway, and the Australia and New Zealand Banking Group.

The Templeton International Stock Fund has an excellent consistency record, having beaten its peer group for 8 of the past 10 years. It also has a very good risk/reward ranking and, during the 2000/2001 bear market, it outperformed the average international equity fund, which posted a return of −19.2%, by 10.9%. Although there is a 1-in-4 chance that returns will be negative over a 3-month period and a 1-in-13 chance they will be negative over a 1-year period, the fund has made money over all 3- and 5-year periods. Looking at all 5-year rolling periods, returns have averaged 15.7%, ranging from a high of 22.3% to a low of 9.1%.

Fund Facts

Fund: TEMPLETON INTERNATIONAL STOCK
Manager: Donald F. Reed
Category: International Equity

Best/Worst Rolling Returns

3-Month Period

Best: 23.4%
Worst: -15.1%
Average: 3.6%
Times fund lost money: 24%

1-Year Period

Best: 52.8%
Worst: -10.1%
Average: 15.8%
Times fund lost money: 8%

3-Year Period

Best: 26.8%
Worst: 1.8%
Average: 15.4%
Times fund lost money: 0%

5-Year Period

Best: 22.3%
Worst: 9.1%
Average: 15.7%
Times fund lost money: 0%

Performance Record

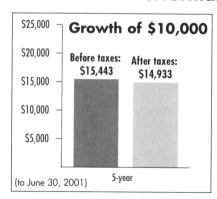

Consistency Record 80%

Risk/Reward Ranking A

Tax-Efficiency Ratio 92%

Fund Details

| Mgmt. Expense Ratio | 2.64% | Sales charges | Yes |
| Minimum RRSP | $500 | Minimum non-RRSP | $500 |

See chapter 13 for a discussion on how to interpret the Fund Facts page.

Chapter 19
U.S. Equity Funds

U.S. equity funds invest in common shares and other equity securities of U.S. companies, with the primary objective of providing long-term capital growth through increases in stock prices. Funds in this category must hold a minimum of 50% of their total assets and 75% of their non-cash assets in equities or equity equivalents of companies located in the United States or in derivatives based on the U.S. market. U.S. equity funds are primarily suitable for investors who seek growth of capital, have an investment time frame of at least 5 years, and are able to accept greater short-term fluctuations in the value of their investment. They are also good for adding diversification to a Canada-only portfolio and as a hedge against any decline in the value of the Canadian dollar. They are unsuitable for those who are unable to assume risk, have an investment time horizon of less than 5 years, or depend on maximizing current income from their investments.

Of the close to 440 U.S. equity funds, only two met the criteria to be included in *Chand's Top 50 Mutual Funds*.

Investors U.S. Large-Cap Value Fund

Family: Investors Group

Tel: 888-746-6344

Web site: www.investorsgroup.com

The Investors U.S. Large-Cap Value Fund was launched in January 1962 and has been managed by Terry Wong since June 1998. Wong, a certified management accountant, has been with the Winnipeg-based Investors Group since 1991. The team approach to managing funds has enabled lead manager Terry Wong to take over the helm of this fund while continuing to deliver consistent above-average performance.

The investment objective of this load fund is to provide long-term capital growth by investing in a concentrated portfolio of U.S. equities. Wong is a value-oriented stock picker who, in choosing likely candidates for the portfolio, zeroes in on companies that typically have strong cash flows and returns on equity of 15% or more, but whose stocks trade at a discount to the S&P 500 Index.

With over $2.4 billion in assets, the fund holds about 35 securities in its portfolio and is heavily weighted in the financial sector, which accounts for 30% of its assets. The fund also has significant weightings in the consumer staples and technology sectors, which together account for another 25% of its assets. Just over 10% of the fund's portfolio is in cash. The fund's top 10 holdings make up about 40% of the portfolio and include Tricon Global Restaurants, AFLAC Inc., Berkshire Hathaway, Sara Lee, and Reebok International.

The Investors U.S. Large-Cap Value Fund has an excellent consistency record, having beaten its peer group for 8 of the past 10 years. It also has an excellent tax-efficiency ratio and a very good risk/reward ranking. During the 2000/2001 bear market, the fund posted a return of 20.0%, outperforming the average U.S. equity fund, which posted a return of –17.3%. Although there is a 1-in-6 chance that returns will be negative over a 3-month period and a 1-in-11 chance they will be negative over a 1-year period, the fund has made money over all 3- and 5-year periods. Looking at all 5-year rolling periods, returns have averaged 20.4%, ranging from a high of 25.2% to a low of 16.0%.

Fund Facts

Fund: INVESTORS U.S. LARGE-CAP VALUE
Manager: Terry Wong
Category: U.S. Equity

Best/Worst Rolling Returns

3-Month Period

Best: 20.9%
Worst: -14.7%
Average: 4.5%
Times fund lost money: 16%

1-Year Period

Best: 54.1%
Worst: -18.0%
Average: 19.1%
Times fund lost money: 9%

3-Year Period

Best: 33.0%
Worst: 7.3%
Average: 19.5%
Times fund lost money: 0%

5-Year Period

Best: 25.2%
Worst: 16.0%
Average: 20.4%
Times fund lost money: 0%

Performance Record

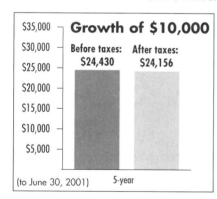

Growth of $10,000
Before taxes: $24,430
After taxes: $24,156
(to June 30, 2001) 5-year

Consistency Record 80%

Risk/Reward Ranking A

Tax-Efficiency Ratio 99%

Fund Details

Mgmt. Expense Ratio	2.94%	Sales charges	Yes
Minimum RRSP	$500	Minimum non-RRSP	$1,000

See chapter 13 for a discussion on how to interpret the Fund Facts page.

McLean Budden American Equity Fund
Family: McLean Budden Limited
Tel: 800-884-0436
Web site: www.mcleanbudden.com

The McLean Budden American Equity Fund was launched in January 1989 and is managed by the company's foreign equity management team. McLean Budden set up shop in 1947 and is one of Canada's oldest investment counselling firms. The company emphasizes a team approach to investing and has a seasoned group of portfolio managers whose average length of experience is over 15 years.

The investment objective of this no-load fund is to provide long-term capital appreciation by investing in the stocks of large- and medium-sized U.S. companies. In making their picks, the managers focus on stocks from the S&P 500 that possess strong earnings growth, proven management, financial strength, business potential, earnings stability, and good return on equity.

With just over $100 million in assets, the fund follows a bottom-up/growth investment style with a large-cap equity bias. The fund holds about 50 securities in its portfolio and is heavily weighted in the technology, financial services, and capital goods sectors, which account for over 50% of its assets. The top 10 holdings make up about 30% of the portfolio and include United Technologies, Proctor & Gamble, American Home Products, Pfizer Inc., and Microsoft.

The McLean Budden American Equity Fund has an excellent risk/reward ranking and, during the 2000/2001 bear market, it outperformed the average U.S. equity fund, which posted a return of –17.3%, by 11.7%. Although there is a 1-in-4 chance that returns will be negative over a 3-month period and a 1-in-50 chance they will be negative over a 1-year period, the fund has made money over all 3- and 5-year periods. Looking at all 5-year rolling periods, returns have averaged 20.1%, ranging from a high of 26.3% to a low of 11.6%. The fund has posted positive returns for each of the past 10 calendar years, with returns ranging from a high of 36.5% in 1997 to a low of 2.8% in 1993.

Fund Facts

Fund:	MCLEAN BUDDEN AMERICAN EQUITY
Manager:	Management team
Category:	U.S. Equity

Best/Worst Rolling Returns

3-Month Period

Best: 26.6%
Worst: -12.1%
Average: 4.1%
Times fund lost money: 26%

1-Year Period

Best: 55.5%
Worst: -1.8%
Average: 17.7%
Times fund lost money: 2%

3-Year Period

Best: 31.6%
Worst: 5.9%
Average: 19.1%
Times fund lost money: 0%

5-Year Period

Best: 26.3%
Worst: 11.6%
Average: 20.1%
Times fund lost money: 0%

Performance Record

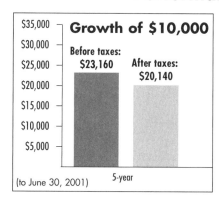

Consistency Record 70%

Risk/Reward Ranking A

Tax-Efficiency Ratio 82%

Fund Details

Mgmt. Expense Ratio	1.30%	Sales charges	No
Minimum RRSP	$10,000	Minimum non-RRSP	$10,000

See chapter 13 for a discussion on how to interpret the Fund Facts page.

Chapter 20
European Equity Funds

The primary objective of European equity funds is to achieve long-term capital growth by investing in the stocks of various domestic European companies. These funds must hold a minimum of 50% of their total assets and 75% of their non-cash assets in equities or equity equivalents of European companies or in derivatives based in developed European equity markets. Moreover, more than one European country must be represented in the portfolio at all times.

European equity funds are suitable for more aggressive investors who seek growth of capital, have an investment time frame of at least 5 years, and are comfortable with short-term, and sometimes significant, fluctuations in the value of their investment. These funds are also good for providing a hedge against any decline in the value of the Canadian dollar and for adding diversification to a North America-only portfolio. However, potential investors should be prepared to assume the additional risks associated with investing in international markets, such as exchange-rate fluctuations. These funds are not suitable for cautious or conservative investors or those with short investment time horizons.

Of the close to 130 European equity funds, only two met the criteria to be included in *Chand's Top 50 Mutual Funds*.

HSBC European Fund
Family: HSBC Investment Funds Canada
Tel: 800-830-8888
Web site: www.hsbc.ca

The HSBC European Fund was launched in October 1994 and has been managed by the HSBC asset management investment team since its inception. The company emphasizes a team approach to fund management and capitalizes on the local knowledge and expertise of its teams of investment professionals located in every major financial market around the world.

The investment objective of this no-load fund is to achieve long-term capital growth by investing primarily in companies whose main operations are located in the major European countries, such as the United Kingdom, Germany, France, and Italy. The fund is managed from London and the managers follow a blended top-down/bottom-up investment approach in selecting stocks for the portfolio.

With close to $140 million in assets, the fund is well-diversified and holds about 110 securities in its portfolio. It has positions in about 15 European countries, with 24% invested in the United Kingdom, 14% in France, and around 9% each in Germany, Italy, and Switzerland. The fund's top 10 holdings make up about 30% of the portfolio and include GlaxoSmithKline, the Vodafone Group, Shell Transport and Trading, BP Amoco, Nestlé, and BNP Paribas.

The HSBC European Fund has an excellent consistency record, having beaten its peer group for 5 of the past 6 years. The fund also has a high tax-efficiency ratio of 91% over 5 years. Although there is a 1-in-3 chance that returns will be negative over a 3-month period and a 1-in-8 chance they will be negative over a 1-year period, the fund has made money over all 3- and 5-year periods. Looking at all 5-year rolling periods, returns have averaged 22.2%, ranging from a high of 27.9% to a low of 15.1%. The fund has posted positive returns for 5 of the past 6 calendar years, with returns ranging from a high of 42.2% in 1998 to a low of –6.8% in 2000, which was above the average for European equity funds.

Fund Facts

Fund:	HSBC EUROPEAN EQUITY
Manager:	Management team
Category:	European Equity

Best/Worst Rolling Returns

3-Month Period

Best: 32.4%
Worst: -12.0%
Average: 4.2%
Times fund lost money: 29%

1-Year Period

Best: 48.6%
Worst: -22.5%
Average: 20.8%
Times fund lost money: 12%

3-Year Period

Best: 33.9%
Worst: 3.4%
Average: 23.9%
Times fund lost money: 0%

5-Year Period

Best: 27.9%
Worst: 15.1%
Average: 22.2%
Times fund lost money: 0%

Performance Record

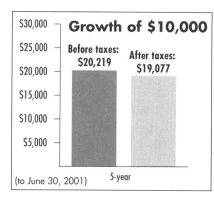

Growth of $10,000

Before taxes: $20,219
After taxes: $19,077

(to June 30, 2001) 5-year

Consistency Record	83%
Risk/Reward Ranking	A
Tax-Efficiency Ratio	91%

Fund Details

Mgmt. Expense Ratio	2.28%	Sales charges	No
Minimum RRSP	$500	Minimum non-RRSP	$500

See chapter 13 for a discussion on how to interpret the Fund Facts page.

Scudder Greater Europe Fund
Family: Scudder Group of Funds
Tel: 888-462-9986
Web site: www.scudder.ca

The Scudder Greater Europe Fund was launched in October 1995 and has been managed by Carol Franklin, Joan Gregory, and Nicholas Bratt since its inception. With over 50 years of combined investment experience, Franklin sets the fund's investment strategy and oversees its daily operation; Gregory, the fund team manager, focusses on investment selection; and Bratt, the director of Scudder's global equity group, is responsible for the firm's overall global equity investment strategies.

This fund, originally sold through the Classic Series as no-load, is now only available through the company's Advisor Series. The objective of this fund is to achieve long-term capital appreciation through investments primarily in European companies. The managers follow a bottom-up/growth-investment strategy and focus on the greater European region. This area encompasses both the industrialized nations of Western Europe and the less-wealthy or less-developed markets in Southern and Eastern Europe.

With $95 million in assets, the fund is well diversified and holds about 90 securities in its portfolio. It has significant positions in a number of European countries, with 25% invested in both the United Kingdom and France, and around 20% in Germany. The fund is heavily concentrated in the financial services, industrial products, and consumer sectors, which together account for about 70% of assets. The top 10 holdings make up just over 20% of the portfolio and include Royal Dutch Petroleum, GlaxoSmithKline, BP Amoco, Nestlé, and the Banque Nationale de Paris.

The Scudder Greater Europe Fund has an excellent consistency record, having beaten its peer group for each of the past 5 years. The fund also has a excellent risk/reward ranking and a tax-efficiency ratio of 96% over 5 years. Although there is a 1-in-3 chance that returns will be negative over a 3-month period and a 1-in-6 chance they will be negative over a 1-year period, the fund has made money over all 3- and 5-year periods. Looking at all 5-year rolling periods, returns have averaged 18.4%, ranging from a high of 21.6% to a low of 14.1%.

Fund Facts

Fund: SCUDDER GREATER EUROPE

Manager: Carol Franklin, Joan Gregory, & Nicholas Bratt

Category: Canadian Equity

Best/Worst Rolling Returns

3-Month Period

Best: 30.9%
Worst: -15.3%
Average: 4.3%
Times fund lost money: 30%

1-Year Period

Best: 60.7%
Worst: -22.3%
Average: 21.2%
Times fund lost money: 18%

3-Year Period

Best: 32.6%
Worst: 0.3%
Average: 21.6%
Times fund lost money: 0%

5-Year Period

Best: 21.6%
Worst: 14.1%
Average: 18.4%
Times fund lost money: 0%

Performance Record

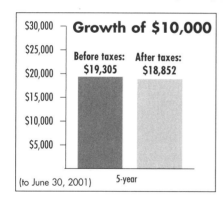

Growth of $10,000

Before taxes: $19,305   After taxes: $18,852

(to June 30, 2001)   5-year

Consistency Record 100%

Risk/Reward Ranking A

Tax-Efficiency Ratio 96%

Fund Details

Mgmt. Expense Ratio	2.90%	Sales charges	Yes
Minimum RRSP	$500	Minimum non-RRSP	$1,000

See chapter 13 for a discussion on how to interpret the Fund Facts page.

Part Five

Fixed Income and Money Market Funds

Introduction

Mutual funds, such as money market, mortgage, and bond, are designed to provide investors with a regular stream of interest income. Money market funds invest principally in short-term (less than one year) debt securities and are designed to give maximum protection to the capital invested. This makes them a good option for short-term investment goals or as an emergency cash fund. However, over the long term, money market funds provide the lowest real rate of return. Bond funds may hold debt obligations with short-term (1-5 years), intermediate-term (5-10 years), or long-term (over 10 years) maturities. Mortgage funds, on the other hand, invest primarily in conventional and insured first mortgages on prime residential properties located across Canada. Bond funds generally offer greater income potential than mortgage funds but, depending on the maturity and quality of the bond fund's holdings, typically carry more risk.

Chapter 21
Canadian Bond Funds

Bond funds typically invest in short-, medium-, and long-term debt securities issued by governments and large corporations. The average term-to-maturity of a Canadian bond fund's portfolio, including short-term investments, must be greater than 3 years. The primary objective of this type of fund is to provide investors with a regular stream of income and some capital-gains potential.

Bond funds generally offer greater income than money market or mortgage funds and are usually less volatile than equity funds. The biggest advantages of bond funds are their liquidity and the diversification you can get with limited amounts of money (funds typically hold between 50 and 300 issues). However, unlike bonds bought individually, bond funds do not have a fixed rate of interest or maturity date (the date when the debt security matures and the amount borrowed by the bond issuer must be paid back). The composition of this type of fund changes constantly due to changing market conditions, the maturing of individual bonds in the portfolio, and the manager's buying and selling decisions. Therefore, interest income payments will fluctuate.

When choosing a bond fund, you should be aware of the risks involved. Credit risk is the possibility that the issuer of the bond will not make the interest payments or repay the principal on maturity. Government of Canada securities are perceived to have virtually no risk, followed by provincial government bonds and high-quality corporate bonds. Issuers with the least credit risk generally offer lower interest rates than higher-risk issuers. Market risk, in the case of bond funds, is the risk that the value of your investment will decrease due to rising interest rates.

All bonds are given a credit quality rating by Standard & Poor's Canadian Bond Rating Service and the Dominion Bond Rating Service. Government of Canada bonds, issued and backed by the federal government, are of the highest credit quality and are considered superior to bonds rated AAA, the highest investment grade rating. This rating is followed in descending order by AA, A, BBB, BB, B, CCC, CC, and C. Junk bonds or high yield bonds are considered to be quite speculative and are rated BB or lower. These higher-risk issues generally offer higher yields.

The performance of bond funds is influenced by interest-rate movements. When interest rates rise, the market price of fixed income securities declines. When interest rates go down, the value of fixed income funds rises and investors enjoy capital appreciation as well as income. Short term bond funds (with average maturities of the bonds held in the fund ranging from 1 to 5 years) have the least risk, followed by intermediate term bond funds (5-10 years), and then long term bond funds (over 10 years).

The longer the average weighted maturity of the bonds held in a portfolio, the more sensitive the fund will be to interest-rate movements (the average weighted maturity is the average length of time until each bond held by a fund reaches maturity and is repaid). For example, investors in a bond fund with an average maturity of 6 years should expect, roughly, a 6% increase in returns for every 1% decline in interest rates. Conversely, if interest rates increase by 1%, returns could decline by as much as 6%. Bond funds with longer average maturities usually offer higher yields because of the higher risk. To help investors find bond funds with a suitable risk level, we provide the average maturity term (the date when the principal is repaid to the bondholder) for each of the top 50 Heavy Hitter bond funds. Bond funds generally have a higher risk than money market and mortgage funds but a lower risk than equity funds.

Bond funds are suitable for investors seeking a regular stream of interest income with the potential for capital gains. They are also a good choice for meeting medium-term financial goals, depending on the maturity and quality of the fund's holdings, and as part of a well-diversified portfolio. These funds are unsuitable for investors with a short investment time horizon or those for whom capital growth is the primary objective.

Of the 260 Canadian bond funds, only eight met the criteria to be included in *Chand's Top 50 Mutual Funds*.

Beutel Goodman Income Fund
Family: Beutel Goodman Managed Funds
Tel: 800-461-4551
Web site: www.beutel-can.com

The Beutel Goodman Income Fund was launched in January 1991 and has been co-managed by the experienced team of Bruce Corneil, David Gregoris, and John Christie since 1992. Corneil, the lead manager, has been in the investment industry for over 26 years; Gregoris, a CFA with an MBA from the University of Windsor, joined Beutel Goodman in 1992; and Christie, a CFA with an MBA from Queen's University, joined the company in 1993.

The investment objective of this load fund is to provide current income while protecting capital by investing primarily in fixed income securities of Canadian government and corporate issuers. In setting the maturity and duration of the portfolio, the managers actively forecast and analyze the direction of the change in interest rates. In order to enhance the yield, the fund invests in high-quality corporate bonds based on the company's in-house research.

With $70 million in assets, the fund invests primarily in intermediate term bonds and has an average duration of just over 6 years. Its portfolio of around 45 securities consists of just over 50% in Government of Canada bonds, just over 25% in corporate bonds, and around 20% in provincial bonds. Close to 50% of the bonds are rated AAA, 20% AA, and the remainder have a credit quality rating of A. Income distributions are made quarterly and capital gains distributions annually.

The Beutel Goodman Income Fund has an excellent risk/reward ranking and a good consistency record, having beaten its peer group for 8 of the past 10 years. Although there is a 1-in-5 chance that returns will be negative over a 3-month period and a 1-in-8 chance they will be negative over a 1-year period, the fund has made money for its investors over all 3- and 5-year periods. Looking at all 5-year rolling periods, returns have averaged 9.0% and ranged from a high of 10.9% to a low of 7.3%.

Fund Facts

Fund:	BEUTEL GOODMAN INCOME
Manager:	Bruce Corneil, David Gregoris, & John Christie
Category:	Canadian Bond

Best/Worst Rolling Returns

3-Month Period

Best: 11.9%
Worst: -9.9%
Average: 2.2%
Times fund lost money: 22%

1-Year Period

Best: 22.6%
Worst: -10.0%
Average: 8.8%
Times fund lost money: 12%

3-Year Period

Best: 14.1%
Worst: 4.2%
Average: 8.3%
Times fund lost money: 0%

5-Year Period

Best: 10.9%
Worst: 7.3%
Average: 9.0%
Times fund lost money: 0%

Performance Record

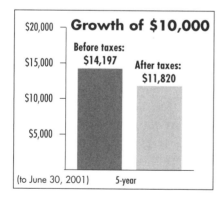

Growth of $10,000
Before taxes: $14,197
After taxes: $11,820
(to June 30, 2001)   5-year

Consistency Record 80%

Risk/Reward Ranking A

Tax-Efficiency Ratio 47%

Fund Details

Mgmt. Expense Ratio	0.67%	Sales charges	Yes
Minimum RRSP	$10,000	Minimum non-RRSP	$10,000

See chapter 13 for a discussion on how to interpret the Fund Facts page.

Bissett Bond Fund

Family: Franklin Templeton Investments
Tel: 800-387-0830
Web site: www.franklintempleton.ca

The Bissett Bond Fund was launched in August 1986 and has been managed by Guy LeBlanc since January 1998. LeBlanc, a CFA with a BBA from the Université du Québec à Montréal, joined Bissett in 1997 and is currently the director of fixed income. Bissett & Associates of Calgary merged with Franklin Templeton Investments in the Fall of 2000.

This fund, originally sold through the F Series as a no-load, is now only available to new investors through the company's Advisor Series. The investment objective of this fund is to provide a high level of current income and some long-term capital appreciation by investing primarily in federal, provincial, and corporate bonds. In selecting securities for the portfolio, LeBlanc typically maintains an overweight position in corporate and provincial bonds rated A or higher, and underweights his position in federal government bonds. LeBlanc also controls risk by staggering the maturities of the bonds in the portfolio, thereby reducing the impact of interest-rate fluctuations.

With over $240 million in assets, the fund invests primarily in intermediate term bonds and has an average term-to-maturity of just over 6 years. Its portfolio of around 40 securities consists of close to 45% in corporate bonds and about 25% each in federal and provincial government bonds. Close to 50% of the bonds are rated AAA, 20% are rated AA, and the remainder have a credit quality rating of A. Income distributions are made monthly and capital gains distributions annually.

The Bissett Bond Fund has both a good risk/reward ranking and consistency record. It has beaten its peer group for 7 of the past 10 years. Although there is a 1-in-5 chance that returns will be negative over a 3-month period and a 1-in-10 chance they will be negative over a 1-year period, the fund has made money for its investors over all 3- and 5-year periods. Looking at all 5-year rolling periods, returns have averaged 9.2% and ranged from a high of 10.8% to a low of 7.0%.

Fund Facts

Fund:	BISSETT BOND
Manager:	Guy LeBlanc
Category:	Canadian Bond

Best/Worst Rolling Returns

3-Month Period

Best: 9.8%
Worst: -7.3%
Average: 2.2%
Times fund lost money: 22%

1-Year Period

Best: 22.1%
Worst: -6.2%
Average: 8.6%
Times fund lost money: 10%

3-Year Period

Best: 14.4%
Worst: 3.6%
Average: 8.5%
Times fund lost money: 0%

5-Year Period

Best: 10.8%
Worst: 7.0%
Average: 9.2%
Times fund lost money: 0%

Performance Record

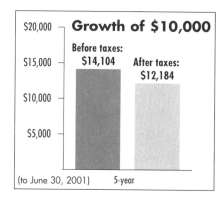

Growth of $10,000

Before taxes: $14,104

After taxes: $12,184

(to June 30, 2001)   5-year

Consistency Record 70%

Risk/Reward Ranking B

Tax-Efficiency Ratio 57%

Fund Details

Mgmt. Expense Ratio	0.80%	Sales charges	Yes
Minimum RRSP	$500	Minimum non-RRSP	$500

See chapter 13 for a discussion on how to interpret the Fund Facts page.

CI Canadian Bond Fund

Family: CI Mutual Funds
Tel: 800-563-5181
Web site: www.cifunds.com

The CI Canadian Bond Fund was launched in January 1993 and has been managed by Jeffrey Herold since its inception. Herold, a CFA with a BComm degree from the University of Toronto, is vice-president and director at J. Zechner Associates Inc., the advisors to the fund. Herold is responsible for the firm's fixed income portfolio management and asset-mix strategy.

The objective of this load fund is to provide investors with a total investment return comprising current income and capital appreciation. The fund invests primarily in government and corporate bonds. In selecting securities for the portfolio, Herold uses a number of techniques such as analyzing the future direction of interest rates, the yield curve, credit and risk ratings, as well as investor sentiment and market conditions.

With over $450 million in assets, the fund invests primarily in intermediate term bonds. Its portfolio of around 30 bond holdings consists of about 64% in Government of Canada bonds, just over 20% in corporate bonds, and around 10% in provincial bonds. Over 90% of the federal government bonds have a maturity of less than 10 years, and about 75% of the corporate bonds have a maturity of less than 10 years. The fund pays out income distributions monthly and capital gains distributions are made annually.

The CI Canadian Bond Fund has an excellent risk/reward ranking and a very good consistency record, having beaten its peer group for 6 of the past 7 years. Although there is a 1-in-4 chance that returns will be negative over a 3-month period and a 1-in-7 chance they will be negative over a 1-year period, the fund has made money for its investors over all 3- and 5-year periods. Looking at all 5-year rolling periods, returns have averaged 8.9% and ranged from a high of 10.7% to a low of 7.0%.

Fund Facts

Fund: CI CANADIAN BOND
Manager: Jeffrey S. Herold
Category: Canadian Bond

Best/Worst Rolling Returns

3-Month Period

Best:	10.4%
Worst:	-5.9%
Average:	1.8%

Times fund lost money: 23%

1-Year Period

Best:	20.2%
Worst:	-4.9%
Average:	7.6%

Times fund lost money: 15%

3-Year Period

Best:	14.6%
Worst:	3.2%
Average:	8.7%

Times fund lost money: 0%

5-Year Period

Best:	10.7%
Worst:	7.0%
Average:	8.9%

Times fund lost money: 0%

Performance Record

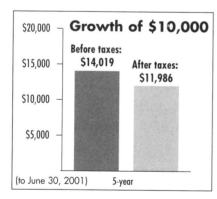

Growth of $10,000

Before taxes: $14,019
After taxes: $11,986

(to June 30, 2001)   5-year

Consistency Record 85%
Risk/Reward Ranking A
Tax-Efficiency Ratio 53%

Fund Details

Mgmt. Expense Ratio	1.71%	Sales charges	Yes
Minimum RRSP	$500	Minimum non-RRSP	$500

See chapter 13 for a discussion on how to interpret the Fund Facts page.

McLean Budden Fixed Income Fund

Family: McLean Budden Limited
Tel: 800-884-0436
Web site: www.mcleanbudden.com

The McLean Budden Fixed Income Fund was launched in January 1989 and and is managed by the company's fixed income management team. McLean Budden set up shop in 1947 and is one of Canada's oldest investment counselling firms. The company emphasizes a team approach to investing and has a seasoned group of portfolio managers whose average length of experience is over 15 years.

The investment objective of this no-load fund is to provide a high level of current income while at the same time minimizing investment risk. The fund invests in a diversified portfolio of high-quality Canadian government and corporate bonds with an average term-to-maturity that typically ranges between 7 to 12 years. In selecting corporate bonds to invest in, the managers choose securities that have received a rating of A or above.

With over $35 million in assets, the fund holds over 60 securities in its portfolio. The fund's assets are almost evenly split with close to 35% in Government of Canada bonds, over 30% in corporate bonds, and just under 30% in provincial bonds. Its top corporate holdings include the Bank of Montreal, CIBC, and the Thomson Corporation, and its top provincial holdings include bonds issued by British Columbia, Ontario, and Quebec. The average term-to-maturity of the fund's bond holdings is just about 8 years. Income distributions are made quarterly and capital gains distributions are made annually.

The McLean Budden Fixed Income Fund has an excellent risk/reward ranking and a good consistency record, having beaten its peer group for 7 of the past 10 years. Although there is a 1-in-5 chance that returns will be negative over a 3-month period and a 1-in-8 chance they will be negative over a 1-year period, the fund has made money for its investors over all 3- and 5-year periods. Looking at all 5-year rolling periods, returns have averaged 9.2% and ranged from a high of 10.7% to a low of 7.5%.

Fund Facts

Fund:	MCLEAN BUDDEN FIXED INCOME
Manager:	Management team
Category:	Canadian Bond

Best/Worst Rolling Returns

3-Month Period

Best: 10.7%
Worst: -8.9%
Average: 2.2%
Times fund lost money: 22%

1-Year Period

Best: 21.6%
Worst: -8.3%
Average: 8.8%
Times fund lost money: 13%

3-Year Period

Best: 14.3%
Worst: 4.3%
Average: 8.5%
Times fund lost money: 0%

5-Year Period

Best: 10.7%
Worst: 7.5%
Average: 9.2%
Times fund lost money: 0%

Performance Record

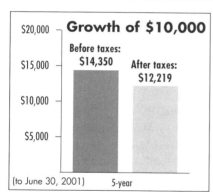

Growth of $10,000
Before taxes: $14,350
After taxes: $12,219
(to June 30, 2001) 5-year

Consistency Record   70%

Risk/Reward Ranking   A

Tax-Efficiency Ratio   55%

Fund Details

Mgmt. Expense Ratio	0.70%	Sales charges	No
Minimum RRSP	$10,000	Minimum non-RRSP	$10,000

See chapter 13 for a discussion on how to interpret the Fund Facts page.

Perigee Index Plus Bond Fund

Family: Perigee Mutual Funds
Tel: 888-437-3333
Web site: www.perigeemutualfunds.com

The Perigee Index Plus Bond Fund was launched in August 1968 and is managed by the company's fixed income management team. Perigee Investment Counsel, which emphasizes a team approach to investing, has been around since the early 1970s and is one of Canada's largest investment firms.

The investment objective of this no-load fund is to provide investors with a steady flow of income. The fund invests in a diversified portfolio of government bonds, high-quality corporate bonds, and mortgage-backed securities guaranteed by the Canada Housing and Mortgage Corporation. In selecting corporate bonds to invest in, the managers minimize risk by choosing securities that have received a credit rating of A or higher. The managers seek to enhance the value of the fund by trading among the different sectors (federal, provincial, municipal, and corporate issues). The fund typically has an average term-to-maturity of 10 years or less.

With over $225 million in assets, the fund holds over 50 securities in its portfolio. About 40% of the fund's portfolio is invested in Government of Canada bonds, and about 30% each in corporate and provincial bonds. Its top corporate holdings include Ontario Hydro and Genesis Trust, and its top provincial holdings include securities issued by Quebec, Ontario, and New Brunswick. The average term-to-maturity of the fund's bond holdings is just over 10 years. Income distributions are made monthly and capital gains distributions are made annually.

The Perigee Index Plus Bond Fund has an excellent consistency record and a good risk/reward ranking. The fund has also beaten its peer group each of the past 10 years. Although there is a 1-in-5 chance that returns will be negative over a 3-month period and a 1-in-10 chance they will be negative over a 1-year period, the fund has made money for its investors over all 3- and 5-year periods. Looking at all 5-year rolling periods, returns have averaged 9.2% and ranged from a high of 11.2% to a low of 7.0%.

Fund Facts

Fund:	PERIGEE INDEX PLUS BOND
Manager:	Management team
Category:	Canadian Bond

Best/Worst Rolling Returns

3-Month Period

Best: 10.1%
Worst: -7.2%
Average: 2.2%
Times fund lost money: 21%

1-Year Period

Best: 21.9%
Worst: -6.1%
Average: 8.8%
Times fund lost money: 10%

3-Year Period

Best: 13.9%
Worst: 3.9%
Average: 8.6%
Times fund lost money: 0%

5-Year Period

Best: 11.2%
Worst: 7.0%
Average: 9.2%
Times fund lost money: 0%

Performance Record

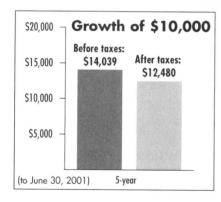

Growth of $10,000
Before taxes: $14,039
After taxes: $12,480
(to June 30, 2001) 5-year

Consistency Record 100%

Risk/Reward Ranking B

Tax-Efficiency Ratio 65%

Fund Details

Mgmt. Expense Ratio	0.75%	Sales charges	No
Minimum RRSP	$2,500	Minimum non-RRSP	$2,500

See chapter 13 for a discussion on how to interpret the Fund Facts page.

PH&N Bond Fund

Family: Phillips, Hager & North Investment Management
Tel: 800-661-6141
Web site: www.phn.ca

The PH&N Bond Fund was launched in December 1970 and is managed by the company's fixed income management team. Phillips, Hager & North, which emphasizes a team approach to investing, has been in business since 1964 and is one of Canada's largest investment firms. The company is well known for a investment philosophy that combines a disciplined approach with a commitment to minimizing risk.

The fundamental objective of this no-load fund is to provide investors with relatively high yields and stability of capital by investing primarily in a well-diversified portfolio of fixed income securities issued by Canadian governments and corporations. In keeping with the company's fixed income investment philosophy, the management team does not make "big bets" on any single strategy, but instead uses a variety of strategies to add value, such as interest rate anticipation and sector allocation.

With over $1.4 billion in assets, the fund holds close to 70 bonds in its portfolio and has an average term-to-maturity of 10.6 years. About 45% of the fund's portfolio is invested in Government of Canada bonds, another 30% is in corporate bonds, and just under 20% is held in provincial bonds. Over 50% of the securities have a credit quality rating of AAA, 15% are rated AA, and the remainder are rated A. Income distributions are made quarterly and capital gains distributions are made annually.

The PH&N Bond Fund has an excellent consistency record and a good risk/reward ranking. The fund has also beaten its peer group in each of the past 10 years. Although there is a 1-in-5 chance that returns will be negative over a 3-month period and a 1-in-11 chance they will be negative over a 1-year period, the fund has made money for its investors over all 3- and 5-year periods. Looking at all 5-year rolling periods, returns have averaged 9.5% and ranged from a high of 11.5% to a low of 7.4%.

Fund Facts

Fund: PH&N BOND
Manager: Management team
Category: Canadian Bond

Best/Worst Rolling Returns

3-Month Period

Best: 10.5%
Worst: -7.8%
Average: 2.3%
Times fund lost money: 21%

1-Year Period

Best: 23.5%
Worst: -6.1%
Average: 9.3%
Times fund lost money: 9%

3-Year Period

Best: 14.0%
Worst: 4.7%
Average: 9.0%
Times fund lost money: 0%

5-Year Period

Best: 11.5%
Worst: 7.4%
Average: 9.5%
Times fund lost money: 0%

Performance Record

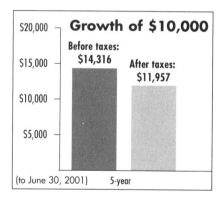

Growth of $10,000
Before taxes: $14,316
After taxes: $11,957
(to June 30, 2001) 5-year

Consistency Record 100%
Risk/Reward Ranking A
Tax-Efficiency Ratio 49%

Fund Details

Mgmt. Expense Ratio	0.58%	Sales charges	No
Minimum RRSP	$25,000	Minimum non-RRSP	$25,000

See chapter 13 for a discussion on how to interpret the Fund Facts page.

Scotia Canadian Income Fund

Family: Scotia Mutual Funds
Tel: 800-268-9269
Web site: www.scotiabank.com

The Scotia Canadian Income Fund was launched in November 1957 and is one of the bank's oldest funds. Scotiabank emphasizes a team approach in the management of their mutual funds, and the Scotia Canadian Income Fund is managed by the fixed income team at Scotia Cassels Investment Counsel, the advisors to the fund.

The investment objective of this no-load fund is to provide a high level of regular interest income combined with modest capital gains. The fund invests primarily in bonds and treasury bills issued by the Government of Canada, provincial and municipal governments, and Canadian corporations. It may also invest in high-quality dividend-paying shares of Canadian corporations. In selecting securities for the portfolio, the managers use a balanced investment strategy that combines a top-down and bottom-up approach.

With over $1.0 billion in assets, the fund holds close to 30 securities in its portfolio and has an average term-to-maturity of just over 10 years. About 50% of the fund's portfolio is invested in Government of Canada bonds, another 30% is in corporate bonds, and around 17% is held in provincial bonds. Its top corporate holdings include Loblaws and General Motors, and its top provincial holdings include securities issued by British Columbia and Ontario. Income distributions are made monthly and capital gains distributions are made annually.

The Scotia Canadian Income Fund has an excellent risk/reward ranking and a good consistency record, having beaten its peer group for 8 of the past 10 years. Although there is a 1-in-5 chance that returns will be negative over a 3-month period and a 1-in-8 chance they will be negative over a 1-year period, the fund has made money for its investors over all 3- and 5-year periods. Looking at all 5-year rolling periods, returns have averaged 9.0% and ranged from a high of 10.7% to a low of 7.1%.

Fund Facts

Fund:	SCOTIA CANADIAN INCOME
Manager:	Management team
Category:	Canadian Bond

Best/Worst Rolling Returns

3-Month Period

Best: 10.5%
Worst: -8.2%
Average: 2.1%
Times fund lost money: 22%

1-Year Period

Best: 22.1%
Worst: -7.9%
Average: 8.6%
Times fund lost money: 13%

3-Year Period

Best: 14.1%
Worst: 4.2%
Average: 8.3%
Times fund lost money: 0%

5-Year Period

Best: 10.7%
Worst: 7.1%
Average: 9.0%
Times fund lost money: 0%

Performance Record

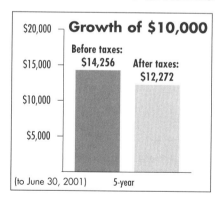

Growth of $10,000

Before taxes: $14,256
After taxes: $12,272

(to June 30, 2001) 5-year

Consistency Record	80%
Risk/Reward Ranking	A
Tax-Efficiency Ratio	57%

Fund Details

Mgmt. Expense Ratio	1.16%	Sales charges	No
Minimum RRSP	$500	Minimum non-RRSP	$500

See chapter 13 for a discussion on how to interpret the Fund Facts page.

TD Canadian Bond Fund
Family: TD Mutual Funds
Tel: 800-268-8166
Web site: www.tdbank.ca

The TD Canadian Bond Fund was launched in June 1988 and has been co-managed by the team of Satish Rai and Paul Gardner since its inception. Rai, a CFA with a BMath degree from the University of Waterloo, has been with the bank since 1986. Gardner, a CFA with a BA in Economics from York University, also joined the bank in 1986.

The objective of this no-load fund is to earn a high rate of interest income through investments in high-quality bonds and debentures issued by the federal, provincial, or municipal governments, and Canadian corporations. In selecting securities for the portfolio, the managers typically overweight corporate bonds in order to provide higher yields and focus on credit analysis in order to reduce risk.

With over $2.2 billion in assets, the fund has about 60% of its portfolio invested in corporate bonds, 30% in federal government bonds, just over 6% in provincial bonds, and the remainder in municipal bonds. The fund holds about 120 securities in its portfolio and its top 10 holdings, which account for about 36% of assets, include the Bank of Nova Scotia, RBC Trust, the province of Ontario, and various federal government bonds of different maturities. The average term-to-maturity of the fund's bond holdings is just over 12 years. Income distributions are made monthly and capital gains distributions are made annually.

The TD Canadian Bond Fund has an excellent risk/reward ranking and a superior consistency record, having beaten its peer group for 9 of the past 10 years. Although there is a 1-in-5 chance that returns will be negative over a 3-month period and a 1-in-10 chance they will be negative over a 1-year period, the fund has made money for its investors over all 3- and 5-year periods. Looking at all 5-year rolling periods, returns have averaged 10.0% and ranged from a high of 11.8% to a low of 8.2%.

Fund Facts

Fund: TD CANADIAN BOND
Manager: Paul Gardner and Satish Rai
Category: Canadian Bond

Best/Worst Rolling Returns

3-Month Period

Best: 10.8%
Worst: -8.8%
Average: 2.4%
Times fund lost money: 22%

1-Year Period

Best: 22.5%
Worst: -8.0%
Average: 9.5%
Times fund lost money: 10%

3-Year Period

Best: 15.8%
Worst: 5.0%
Average: 10.0%
Times fund lost money: 0%

5-Year Period

Best: 11.8%
Worst: 8.2%
Average: 10.0%
Times fund lost money: 0%

Performance Record

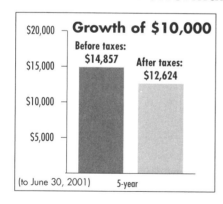

Growth of $10,000
Before taxes: $14,857
After taxes: $12,624
$20,000 / $15,000 / $10,000 / $5,000
(to June 30, 2001) 5-year

Consistency Record 90%

Risk/Reward Ranking A

Tax-Efficiency Ratio 58%

Fund Details

Mgmt. Expense Ratio	1.00%	Sales charges	No
Minimum RRSP	$100	Minimum non-RRSP	$1,000

See chapter 13 for a discussion on how to interpret the Fund Facts page.

Chapter 22

Canadian Short Term Bond Funds

These funds typically invest in Canadian bonds, mortgage-backed securities, and guaranteed investment certificates. The average term-to-maturity of a Canadian short term bond fund's portfolio is generally 1 year to 5 years. These funds are designed to provide investors not only with regular interest payments but also with the potential for some capital gains. Canadian short term bonds are suitable for investors with a low risk tolerance and a mid-term investment time horizon. These funds are unsuitable for investors whose primary objective is growth of capital.

Of the 45 Canadian short term bond funds, only two met the criteria to be included in *Chand's Top 50 Mutual Funds*.

PH&N Short Term Bond & Mortgage Fund
Family: Phillips, Hager & North Investment Management
Tel: 800-661-6141
Web site: www.phn.ca

The PH&N Short Term Bond & Mortgage Fund was launched in December 1993 and is managed by the company's fixed income management team. Phillips, Hager & North, which emphasizes a team approach to investing, has been in business since 1964 and is one of Canada's largest investment firms. The company is well known for an investment philosophy that combines a disciplined approach with a commitment to minimizing risk.

The investment objective of this no-load fund is to provide relatively high yields and stability of capital by investing in Canadian government and corporate bonds, conventional first mortgages, and government-guaranteed mortgages with shorter maturities. In keeping with the company's fixed income investment philosophy, the management team does not make "big bets" on any single strategy, but instead uses a variety of strategies to add value, such as interest-rate anticipation and sector allocation.

With $275 million in assets, the fund invests primarily in short-term securities and has an average term-to-maturity of just under 3 years. Its portfolio of around 60 securities consists of about 45% in corporate bonds, 25% in mortgages, about 20% in federal bonds, with the remainder invested in provincial bonds. Close to 30% of the bonds are rated AAA, 15% are rated AA, and the remainder have a credit quality rating of A. Income distributions are made quarterly and capital gains distributions are made annually.

The PH&N Short Term Bond & Mortgage Fund has an excellent risk/reward ranking and an outstanding consistency record. The fund has beaten its peer group for each of the past 10 years. Although there is a 1-in-9 chance that returns will be negative over a 3-month period and a 1-in-33 chance they will be negative over a 1-year period, the fund has made money for its investors over all 3- and 5-year periods. Looking at all 5-year rolling periods, returns have averaged 7.0% and ranged from a high of 8.3% to a low of 6.2%.

Fund Facts

Fund:	PH&N SHORT TERM BOND & MORTAGE
Manager:	Management team
Category:	Canadian Short Term Bond

Best/Worst Rolling Returns

3-Month Period

Best: 6.1%
Worst: -5.0%
Average: 1.6%
Times fund lost money: 11%

1-Year Period

Best: 16.3%
Worst: -2.0%
Average: 7.2%
Times fund lost money: 3%

3-Year Period

Best: 10.5%
Worst: 3.9%
Average: 7.0%
Times fund lost money: 0%

5-Year Period

Best: 8.3%
Worst: 6.2%
Average: 7.0%
Times fund lost money: 0%

Performance Record

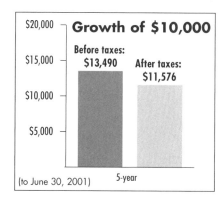

Growth of $10,000

Before taxes: $13,490
After taxes: $11,576

(to June 30, 2001)   5-year

Consistency Record	100%
Risk/Reward Ranking	A
Tax-Efficiency Ratio	48%

Fund Details

Mgmt. Expense Ratio	0.62%	Sales charges	No
Minimum RRSP	$25,000	Minimum non-RRSP	$25,000

See chapter 13 for a discussion on how to interpret the Fund Facts page.

Talvest Income Fund

Family: Talvest Mutual Funds
Tel: 800-268-0081
Web site: www.talvest.com

The Talvest Income Fund was launched in October 1974 and has been managed by Jeffrey Waldman since 1998. Waldman has over 12 years of experience managing bond portfolios, and is the vice-president of the fixed income division at TAL Global Asset Management—the advisor to the fund.

The investment objective of this load fund is to provide a high level of interest income while protecting capital by investing in Canadian government and high quality corporate bonds, conventional first mortgages, and mortgage-backed securities guaranteed by the Government of Canada. In selecting corporate bonds for the portfolio, Waldman focusses on securities that are attractively priced, offer good quality, and have passed the firm's internal credit research and analysis.

With over $65 million in assets, the fund invests primarily in short-term securities and has an average term-to-maturity of about $3\frac{1}{2}$ years. Over 85% of the portfolio's bond component is invested in short-term securities, and another 15% is in medium-term bonds. The fund holds around 15 securities with about 35% of assets invested in mortgages, 30% in corporate bonds, 15% in provincial bonds, and the remainder in federal bonds. Income distributions are made monthly and capital gains distributions are made annually.

The Talvest Income Fund has both a good risk/reward ranking and a good consistency record. The fund has beaten its peer group for 7 of the past 10 years. Although there is a 1-in-6 chance that returns will be negative over a 3-month period and a 1-in-20 chance they will be negative over a 1-year period, the fund has made money for its investors over all 3- and 5-year periods. Looking at all 5-year rolling periods, returns have averaged 6.7% and ranged from a high of 8.8% to a low of 5.1%.

Fund Facts

Fund: TALVEST INCOME
Manager: Jeffrey M. Waldman
Category: Canadian Short Term Bond

Best/Worst Rolling Returns

3-Month Period

Best: 7.2%
Worst: -5.6%
Average: 1.7%
Times fund lost money: 17%

1-Year Period

Best: 16.2%
Worst: -3.9%
Average: 6.6%
Times fund lost money: 5%

3-Year Period

Best: 9.7%
Worst: 2.6%
Average: 6.3%
Times fund lost money: 0%

5-Year Period

Best: 8.8%
Worst: 5.1%
Average: 6.7%
Times fund lost money: 0%

Performance Record

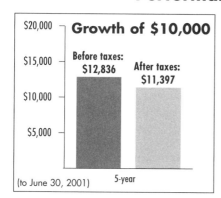

Growth of $10,000

Before taxes: $12,836
After taxes: $11,397

(to June 30, 2001)   5-year

Consistency Record   70%

Risk/Reward Ranking   B

Tax-Efficiency Ratio   52%

Fund Details

Mgmt. Expense Ratio	1.69%	Sales charges	Yes
Minimum RRSP	$500	Minimum non-RRSP	$500

See chapter 13 for a discussion on how to interpret the Fund Facts page.

Chapter 23
Canadian Mortgage Funds

Most mortgage funds invest in conventional and insured first mortgages on prime residential properties located in major cities across Canada. Some funds also include commercial properties in their portfolios. As mortgage funds typically produce a rate of income that is in line with mortgage interest rates, these funds are suitable for conservative investors seeking additional current income. However, because fund managers rarely trade the mortgages they hold, capital-gains potential is low. Next to money market funds, mortgage funds are the least risky type of mutual fund. These funds are unsuitable for investors whose primary objective is growth of capital.

Of the over 25 Canadian mortgage funds, only one met the criteria to be included in *Chand's Top 50 Mutual Funds*.

HSBC Mortgage Fund

Family: HSBC Investment Funds Canada
Tel: 800-830-8888
Web site: www.hsbc.ca

The HSBC Mortgage Fund was launched in October 1992 and has been managed by the HSBC asset management investment team since its inception. The company emphasizes a team approach to fund management and capitalizes on the knowledge and expertise of its teams of investment professionals, located in every major financial market around the world.

The investment objective of this no-load fund is to provide investors with a high level of monthly income and capital growth over the medium and long term, while at the same time protecting capital. The fund invests primarily in residential first mortgages on properties located across Canada and may also invest in other short-term securities. With close to $140 million in assets, about 90% of the fund's portfolio is invested in mortgages and the remainder is in treasury bills and short-term corporate notes. Income distributions are made monthly and capital gains distributions are made annually.

The HSBC Mortgage Fund has both an excellent risk/reward ranking and consistency record. The fund has beaten its peer group for 7 of the past 8 years. Although there is a 1-in-9 chance that returns will be negative over a 3-month period, the fund has made money for its investors over all 1-, 3-, and 5-year periods. Looking at all 5-year rolling periods, returns have averaged 6.8% and ranged from a high of 8.6% to a low of 5.4%. The fund has posted positive returns for each of the past 8 calendar years, with returns ranging from a high of 13.3% in 1995 to a low of 2.0% in 1999.

Fund Facts

Fund:	HSBC MORTGAGE
Manager:	Management team
Category:	Canadian Mortgage

Best/Worst Rolling Returns

3-Month Period

Best: 6.3%
Worst: -1.6%
Average: 1.7%
Times fund lost money: 11%

1-Year Period

Best: 16.4%
Worst: 1.0%
Average: 7.0%
Times fund lost money: 0%

3-Year Period

Best: 10.3%
Worst: 3.4%
Average: 6.8%
Times fund lost money: 0%

5-Year Period

Best: 8.6%
Worst: 5.4%
Average: 6.8%
Times fund lost money: 0%

Performance Record

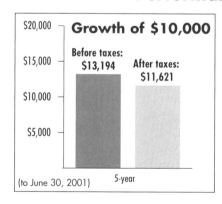

Growth of $10,000
Before taxes: $13,194
After taxes: $11,621
(to June 30, 2001) 5-year

Consistency Record	88%
Risk/Reward Ranking	A
Tax-Efficiency Ratio	53%

Fund Details

Mgmt. Expense Ratio	1.63%	Sales charges	No
Minimum RRSP	$500	Minimum non-RRSP	$500

See chapter 13 for a discussion on how to interpret the Fund Facts page.

Chapter 24
Canadian Money Market Funds

Money market funds typically invest in low-risk, high-quality corporate and government short-term debt securities and government-guaranteed Canadian treasury bills. The primary objectives of these funds are to provide income based on general interest rates and to give maximum protection to the capital invested. To date, none of these funds has ever lost money, and unlike other mutual funds, the unit price of money market funds is regulated to remain fixed at $10. This makes them a good option for short-term investment goals or as an emergency cash fund. However, over the long term, these funds provide the lowest real rate of return. They also add a conservative cushion to a diversified portfolio. This type of fund is suitable for investors primarily seeking security of capital and liquidity. They are unsuitable for investors seeking the potential for long-term growth through capital appreciation.

Of the close to 200 Canadian money market funds, only two met the criteria to be included in *Chand's Top 50 Mutual Funds*.

Elliott & Page Money Fund

Family: Elliott & Page Mutual Funds

Tel: 888-588-7999

Web site: www.elliottandpage.com

The Elliott & Page Money Fund was launched in July 1984 and has been managed by Maralyn Kobayashi since its inception. A vice-president of the firm with over 30 years of investment experience, Kobayashi is the lead portfolio manager of all Canadian and U.S. cash accounts at Elliott & Page.

The investment objective of this fund is to provide investors with a high level of interest income combined with safety of principal and maintenance of liquidity. The fund invests in high-quality, short-term fixed income securities, issued by the federal or provincial governments, Canadian chartered banks, and loan or trust companies operating in Canada. The overall portfolio has an average term-to-maturity of 87 days. Income distributions are made monthly.

The Elliott & Page Money Fund, with over $490 million in assets, has both an excellent risk/reward ranking and consistency record, having beaten its peer group for each of the past 10 years. The fund has made money for its investors over all 3-month, 1-, 3-, and 5-year periods. Looking at all 5-year rolling periods, returns have averaged 4.6% and ranged from a high of 5.9% to a low of 4.1%. The fund has posted positive returns for each of the past 10 calendar years, with returns ranging from a high of 10.5% in 1991 to a low of 2.6% in 1997.

Fund Facts

Fund: ELLIOTT & PAGE MONEY
Manager: Maralyn Kobayashi
Category: Canadian Money Market

Best/Worst Rolling Returns

3-Month Period

Best: 2.6%
Worst: 0.4%
Average: 1.2%
Times fund lost money: 0%

1-Year Period

Best: 8.5%
Worst: 2.4%
Average: 4.8%
Times fund lost money: 0%

3-Year Period

Best: 6.0%
Worst: 3.5%
Average: 4.6%
Times fund lost money: 0%

5-Year Period

Best: 5.9%
Worst: 4.1%
Average: 4.6%
Times fund lost money: 0%

Performance Record

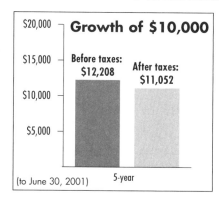

Growth of $10,000
Before taxes: $12,208
After taxes: $11,052
(to June 30, 2001) 5-year

Consistency Record 100%

Risk/Reward Ranking A

Tax-Efficiency Ratio 50%

Fund Details

Mgmt. Expense Ratio	0.91%	Sales charges	No
Minimum RRSP	$500	Minimum non-RRSP	$500

See chapter 13 for a discussion on how to interpret the Fund Facts page.

Mackenzie Cash Management Fund

Family: Mackenzie Financial Corporation

Tel: 800-387-0614

Web site: www.mackenziefinancial.com

The Mackenzie Cash Management Fund was launched in July 1984 and has been managed by the firm's fixed income team since its inception. The team manages a combined total of over $2 billion in fixed income assets.

The investment objective of the fund is to provide investors with a steady flow of interest income combined with safety of capital and maintenance of liquidity. The fund invests mainly in money market securities including treasury bills, commercial paper, and banker's acceptances. It also invests in bonds with maturities of up to 1 year, issued by corporations and the federal and provincial governments. The managers reduce risk by keeping the maturities of most of the fund's investments within 30 to 90 days. Income distributions are made monthly.

The Mackenzie Cash Management Fund, with over $510 million in assets, has an excellent risk/reward ranking and consistency record, having beaten its peer group for each of the past 10 years. The fund has made money for its investors over all 3-month, 1-, 3-, and 5-year periods. Looking at all 5-year rolling periods, returns have averaged 4.6% and ranged from a high of 5.7% to a low of 4.1%. The fund has posted positive returns for each of the past 10 calendar years, with returns ranging from a high of 9.1% in 1991 to a low of 2.6% in 1997.

Fund Facts

Fund: MACKENZIE CASH MANAGEMENT
Manager: Management team
Category: Canadian Money Market

Best/Worst Rolling Returns

3-Month Period

Best: 2.0%
Worst: 0.6%
Average: 1.2%
Times fund lost money: 0%

1-Year Period

Best: 7.2%
Worst: 2.6%
Average: 4.8%
Times fund lost money: 0%

3-Year Period

Best: 5.6%
Worst: 3.6%
Average: 4.6%
Times fund lost money: 5%

5-Year Period

Best: 5.7%
Worst: 4.1%
Average: 4.6%
Times fund lost money: 0%

Performance Record

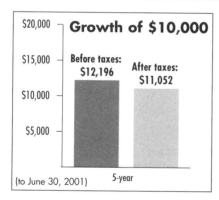

Growth of $10,000

Before taxes: $12,196   After taxes: $11,052

(to June 30, 2001)   5-year

Consistency Record 100%

Risk/Reward Ranking B

Tax-Efficiency Ratio 50%

Fund Details

Mgmt. Expense Ratio	0.54%	Sales charges	Yes
Minimum RRSP	$500	Minimum non-RRSP	$500

See chapter 13 for a discussion on how to interpret the Fund Facts page.

Chapter 25
Foreign Bond Funds

The primary objective of foreign bond funds is to provide a combination of income and the opportunity for capital appreciation, through investing selectively in government and corporate bonds worldwide. These funds seek opportunities around the world by investing in countries where interest rates are high and in countries where there is the prospect of capital appreciation due to falling interest rates. In addition to being susceptible to the general risks inherent with investing in the bond market, these funds will also be influenced by exchange-rate fluctuations. When the Canadian dollar falls in value against the currency of the country in which your fund holds assets, you gain. When the dollar goes up in value, this will eat into your returns. Foreign bond funds are suitable for investors who seek additional income, combined with the opportunity for capital gains, and investors who are looking for a hedge against any decline in the Canadian dollar. They are also suitable for investors wishing to add further diversification to their investment porfolios. Foreign bond funds are unsuitable for investors with short investment time horizons or those who are uncomfortable with the risks inherent in investing in overseas markets.

Of the 90 foreign bond funds, only two met the criteria to be included in *Chand's Top 50 Mutual Funds*.

GGOF Guardian RSP Foreign Income Fund

Family: GGOF Guardian Group of Funds

Tel: 800-668-7327

Web site: www.guardianfunds.com

The GGOF Guardian RSP Foreign Income Fund was launched in July 1994 and has been managed by Laurence Linklater since its inception. As senior portfolio manager, Linklater is responsible for North American bond market and economic research with Dresdner RCM Global Investors, the advisors to the fund. Dresdner is a globally focussed investment company with $120 billion of assets under management.

The investment objective of this load fund is to provide a high level of current income combined with some capital appreciation. The fund invests in bonds and debentures denominated in foreign currencies that are issued by Canadian corporations, the federal or provincial governments, and by certain supranational entities such as the World Bank. The manager reduces risk by diversifying internationally and maintaining a high-quality portfolio with an average credit rating of AAA. By using derivatives to gain exposure to foreign bond markets, the fund is also 100% RSP eligible.

With just under $15 million in assets, the fund holds about 30 securities in its portfolio. Geographically, close to 55% of the fund's assets are invested in Canada, 25% in the United States, 11% in Germany, and around 4% each in France and Japan. Income and capital gains distributions are made quarterly.

The GGOF Guardian RSP Foreign Income Fund has both an excellent risk/reward ranking and consistency record, having beaten its peer group over each of the past 6 years. Although there is a 1-in-3 chance that returns will be negative over any 3-month period and a 1-in-6 chance that they will be negative over a 1-year period, the fund has made money for its investors over all 3- and 5-year periods. Looking at all 5-year rolling periods, returns have averaged 7.2% and ranged from a high of 9.1% to a low of 5.8%.

Fund Facts

Fund:	GGOF GUARDIAN RSP FOREIGN INCOME
Manager:	Laurence Linklater
Category:	Foreign Bond

Best/Worst Rolling Returns

3-Month Period

Best: 10.4%
Worst: -6.0%
Average: 1.8%
Times fund lost money: 31%

1-Year Period

Best: 24.3%
Worst: -10.2%
Average: 7.5%
Times fund lost money: 17%

3-Year Period

Best: 14.7%
Worst: 1.2%
Average: 8.3%
Times fund lost money: 0%

5-Year Period

Best: 9.1%
Worst: 5.8%
Average: 7.2%
Times fund lost money: 0%

Performance Record

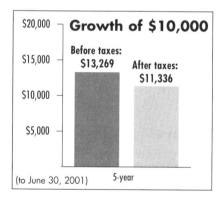

Growth of $10,000

Before taxes: $13,269
After taxes: $11,336

(to June 30, 2001) 5-year

Consistency Record 100%

Risk/Reward Ranking A

Tax-Efficiency Ratio 44%

Fund Details

Mgmt. Expense Ratio	1.90%	Sales charges	Yes
Minimum RRSP	$500	Minimum non-RRSP	$500

See chapter 13 for a discussion on how to interpret the Fund Facts page.

Scotia CanAm US$ Income Fund
Family: Scotia Mutual Funds
Tel: 800-268-9269
Web site: www.scotiabank.com

The Scotia CanAm US$ Income Fund was launched in November 1991 and has been managed since its inception by the fixed income team at Scotia Cassels Investment Counsel, the advisors to the fund. Scotiabank follows a team approach to the management of their mutual funds.

The investment objective of this no-load fund is to provide investors with a high level of interest income. The fund invests primarily in bonds and treasury bills that are denominated in U.S. dollars and issued by federal, provincial, and municipal governments, Canadian corporations, and supranational entities such as the World Bank. Around 60% of the portfolio is invested in short-term securities, 35% is in medium-term securities, and a further 5% is in long-term securities. The average term-to-maturity of the portfolio is just under 5 years. The fund is 100% RSP eligible.

With $26 million in assets, the fund holds about 30 securities in its portfolio. About 65% of assets are invested in federal and provincial government bonds, just over 25% is in corporate debentures, and the remainder is in cash. Income distributions are made monthly and capital gains distributions are made annually.

The Scotia CanAm US$ Income Fund has an excellent risk/reward ranking and a good consistency record, having beaten its peer group for 7 of the past 9 years. Although there is a 1-in-4 chance that returns will be negative over any 3-month period and a 1-in-8 chance that they will be negative over a 1-year period, the fund has made money for its investors over all 3- and 5-year periods. Looking at all 5-year rolling periods, returns have averaged 7.4% and ranged from a high of 8.9% to a low of 5.4%.

Fund Facts

Fund:	SCOTIA CANAM US$ INCOME
Manager:	Management team
Category:	Foreign Bond

Best/Worst Rolling Returns

3-Month Period

Best: 10.6%
Worst: -4.3%
Average: 2.1%
Times fund lost money: 26%

1-Year Period

Best: 22.3%
Worst: -8.4%
Average: 8.1%
Times fund lost money: 12%

3-Year Period

Best: 12.5%
Worst: 4.0%
Average: 7.5%
Times fund lost money: 0%

5-Year Period

Best: 8.9%
Worst: 5.4%
Average: 7.4%
Times fund lost money: 0%

Performance Record

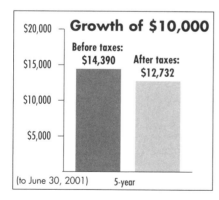

Growth of $10,000
Before taxes: $14,390
After taxes: $12,732
$20,000
$15,000
$10,000
$5,000
(to June 30, 2001)   5-year

Consistency Record 78%

Risk/Reward Ranking A

Tax-Efficiency Ratio 66%

Fund Details

Mgmt. Expense Ratio	1.89%	Sales charges	No
Minimum RRSP	$500	Minimum non-RRSP	$500

See chapter 13 for a discussion on how to interpret the Fund Facts page.

Part 6
Growth and Income Funds

Introduction

Growth and income funds include balanced, asset allocation, and dividend funds. The objective of these funds is to provide investors with long-term capital growth through increases in stock prices, combined with a regular stream of interest or dividend income. Growth and income funds are suitable for individuals who seek a combination of growth of capital and regular income in one fund and who have an investment time horizon of at least 5 years.

The top funds listed here cover a selection of dividend, balanced, asset allocation, and global balanced and asset allocation funds. From among this select group of overachievers, investors will be able to find funds for their portfolios that suit their specific investment objectives and risk tolerance.

Chapter 26
Canadian Balanced Funds

Canadian balanced funds invest in a well-diversified portfolio of various asset classes, including cash and cash equivalents, bonds issued by federal, provincial, and municipal governments and large corporations, and stocks of Canadian companies. These funds are restricted to holding no more than 75% of their portfolio in stocks and no less than 25% in each of bonds and stocks. The investment objective of blanced funds is to provide long-term growth of capital with some income. By investing in a mix of stocks and bonds, balanced funds are less volatile than funds that invest solely in the stock market. Canadian balanced funds are suitable for investors with limited dollars and first-time or cautious investors seeking growth of capital with some income to act as a buffer in declining markets. These funds are also a good choice for investors who want exposure to all the asset classes in one fund. They are unsuitable for investors with a short investment time horizon or those seeking security of capital.

Of the 435 Canadian balanced funds, only three met the criteria to be included in *Chand's Top 50 Mutual Funds*.

Bissett Retirement Fund

Family: Franklin Templeton Investments
Tel: 800-387-0830
Web site: www.franklintempleton.ca

The Bissett Retirement Fund was launched in July 1991 and has been managed by Michael Quinn since 1994. Quinn, a CFA with 20 years of experience, is a vice-president of fixed income and a member of the firm's investment committee. Bissett & Associates of Calgary merged with Franklin Templeton Investments in the Fall of 2000.

This fund, originally sold through the F Series as a no-load, is now only available to new investors through the company's Advisor Series. The objective of this fund is to provide a combination of income and long-term growth of capital. The fund invests only in units of the other Bissett funds and is designed to achieve a balance of fixed income and equity investments. The fixed income component provides capital stability and income while the equity component is intended to provide superior returns over time. Quinn makes changes to the fund's asset allocation depending upon general market conditions and the prospects of the funds held within the portfolio.

With close to $250 million in assets, the fund invests in other Bissett funds with about 60% in equities and 40% in fixed income. On the equity side, Bissett's Canadian Equity Fund accounts for 31%, the American Equity Fund accounts for close to 12%, and the Multinational Growth Fund and the International Equity Trust account for around 6% each. Bissett's Large-Cap, Small-Cap, and Micro-Cap Funds account for another 6% of the portfolio. On the fixed income side, the Bissett Bond Fund accounts for about 40% of assets.

The Bissett Retirement Fund has both an excellent risk/reward ranking and consistency record. The fund has beaten its peer group for 8 of the past 9 years. Although there is a 1-in-5 chance that returns will be negative over a 3-month period and a 1-in-11 chance they will be negative over a 1-year period, the fund has made money over all 3- and 5-year periods. Looking at all 5-year rolling periods, returns have averaged 13.6% and ranged from a high of 17.0% to a low of 10.7%.

Fund Facts

Fund: BISSETT RETIREMENT
Manager: Michael A. Quinn
Category: Canadian Balanced

Best/Worst Rolling Returns

3-Month Period

Best: 13.4%
Worst: -12.1%
Average: 2.9%
Times fund lost money: 22%

1-Year Period

Best: 34.7%
Worst: -5.3%
Average: 12.4%
Times fund lost money: 9%

3-Year Period

Best: 21.6%
Worst: 3.8%
Average: 12.4%
Times fund lost money: 0%

5-Year Period

Best: 17.0%
Worst: 10.7%
Average: 13.6%
Times fund lost money: 0%

Performance Record

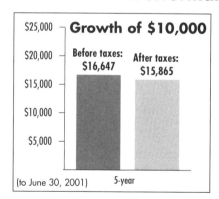

Growth of $10,000

Before taxes: $16,647
After taxes: $15,865

(to June 30, 2001) 5-year

Consistency Record 89%

Risk/Reward Ranking A

Tax-Efficiency Ratio 90%

Fund Details

Mgmt. Expense Ratio	1.45%	Sales charges	Yes
Minimum RRSP	$500	Minimum non-RRSP	$500

See chapter 13 for a discussion on how to interpret the Fund Facts page.

Mackenzie Ivy Growth and Income Fund

Family: Mackenzie Financial Corporation
Tel: 800-387-0614
Web site: www.mackenziefinancial.com

The Mackenzie Ivy Growth and Income Fund was launched in October 1992 and is co-managed by Jerry Javasky and Chuck Roth—a team with over 30 years of combined investment management experience. Javasky, a chartered accountant with an MBA from York University, has been with the fund since May 1997; Roth, a CFA, joined in 1999. Javasky and Roth are also the co-managers of the Mackenzie Ivy Canadian Fund, another top 50 Heavy Hitter fund.

The investment objective of this load fund is to provide a combination of income and long-term growth of capital. To achieve this objective, the managers invest in both fixed income securities, such as Canadian government and corporate bonds and debentures, and in stocks of Canadian and global companies. On the equity side, Javasky and Roth make no attempt to forecast short-term market movements but instead follow a classic buy-and-hold investment style that is a blend of value and growth.

With close to $3 billion in assets, about 65% of the fund's assets is invested in stocks and 35% is in fixed income securities including cash. The fund holds about 60 stocks and close to 15 bonds in its portfolio. On the equity side, about 40% of the fund's assets is invested in the stocks of Canadian companies and about 20% in the United States. The top equity holdings include Berkshire Hathaway, George Weston Ltd., the McGraw-Hill Company, and the Royal Bank of Canada.

The Mackenzie Ivy Growth and Income Fund has an excellent risk/reward ranking and a solid consistency record. The fund has beaten its peer group for 6 of the past 8 years. Although there is a 1-in-5 chance that returns will be negative over a 3-month period and a 1-in-11 chance they will be negative over a 1-year period, the fund has made money for its investors over all 3- and 5-year periods. Looking at all 5-year rolling periods, returns have averaged 12.9%, ranging from a high of 14.4% to a low of 11.0%.

Fund Facts

Fund:	MACKENZIE IVY GROWTH AND INCOME
Manager:	Jerry Javasky and Chuck Roth
Category:	Canadian Balanced

Best/Worst Rolling Returns

3-Month Period

Best: 11.9%
Worst: -9.2%
Average: 2.6%
Times fund lost money: 18%

1-Year Period

Best: 27.9%
Worst: -2.2%
Average: 11.4%
Times fund lost money: 9%

3-Year Period

Best: 20.4%
Worst: 5.2%
Average: 12.4%
Times fund lost money: 0%

5-Year Period

Best: 14.4%
Worst: 11.0%
Average: 12.9%
Times fund lost money: 0%

Performance Record

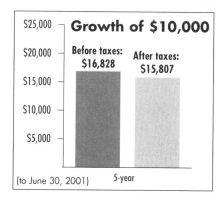

Growth of $10,000
Before taxes: $16,828
After taxes: $15,807
(to June 30, 2001) 5-year

Consistency Record 75%

Risk/Reward Ranking A

Tax-Efficiency Ratio 87%

Fund Details

Mgmt. Expense Ratio	2.20%	Sales charges	Yes
Minimum RRSP	$500	Minimum non-RRSP	$500

See chapter 13 for a discussion on how to interpret the Fund Facts page.

PH&N Balanced Fund

Family: Phillips, Hager & North Investment Management
Tel: 800-661-6141
Web site: www.phn.ca

The PH&N Balanced Fund was launched in September 1991 and is managed by the company's equity and fixed income management teams. Phillips, Hager & North, which emphasizes a team approach to investing, has been in business since 1964 and is one of Canada's largest investment firms. The company is well known for an investment philosophy that combines a disciplined approach with a commitment to minimizing risk.

The investment objective of this fund is to provide for long-term growth and interest income by investing in a balanced portfolio of primarily Canadian common stocks, bonds, treasury bills, and short-term notes. The fund may also invest up to 30% of its assets in foreign securities. About 60% of the portfolio is invested in stocks, another 35% is in fixed income securities, and the remainder is in cash.

With $785 million in assets, the fund is well-diversified and holds about 280 stocks and close to 60 bonds. Geographically, close to 75% of the assets are invested in Canada, 15% in the United States, another 8% in Europe, and about 3% in Japan. Holdings are heavily concentrated in the financial services and industrial products sectors, which together account for about 38% of the portfolio. On the equity side, top holdings include the Royal Bank of Canada, Manulife Financial Corporation, Alberta Energy, and CIBC.

The PH&N Balanced Fund has a good risk/reward ranking and an excellent consistency record, having beaten its peer group for each of the past 10 years. Although there is a 1-in-4 chance that returns will be negative over a 3-month period and a 1-in-20 chance they will be negative over a 1-year period, the fund has made money for its investors over all 3- and 5-year periods. Looking at all 5-year rolling periods, returns have averaged 12.0% and ranged from a high of 14.4% to a low of 9.0%.

Fund Facts

Fund:	PH&N BALANCED
Manager:	Management team
Category:	Canadian Balanced

Best/Worst Rolling Returns

3-Month Period

Best: 12.4%
Worst: -12.1%
Average: 2.6%
Times fund lost money: 25%

3-Year Period

Best: 16.9%
Worst: 4.6%
Average: 11.3%
Times fund lost money: 0%

1-Year Period

Best: 29.2%
Worst: -5.5%
Average: 11.3%
Times fund lost money: 5%

5-Year Period

Best: 14.4%
Worst: 9.0%
Average: 12.0%
Times fund lost money: 0%

Performance Record

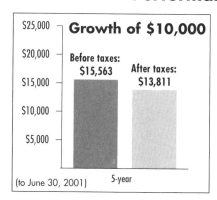

Growth of $10,000
Before taxes: $15,563
After taxes: $13,811
(to June 30, 2001)   5-year

Consistency Record	100%
Risk/Reward Ranking	B
Tax-Efficiency Ratio	72%

Fund Details

Mgmt. Expense Ratio	0.92%	Sales charges	No
Minimum RRSP	$25,000	Minimum non-RRSP	$25,000

See chapter 13 for a discussion on how to interpret the Fund Facts page.

Chapter 27
Canadian Tactical Asset Allocation Funds

Canadian tactical asset allocation funds invest in a well-diversified portfolio of various asset classes, including cash and cash equivalents, bonds, and stocks. These funds have no restrictions on the mix of assets held and will allocate their assets depending upon various factors such as market outlooks and conditions. This type of fund is suitable for investors with an investment time horizon of at least 5 years who want exposure to all the asset classes in one fund but who don't want the added chore of deciding when to move money from one class to another (from stocks to bonds, for instance). Canadian tactical asset allocation funds are unsuitable for short-term investors or those who require a regular stream of income.

Of the 85 Canadian tactical asset allocation funds, only two met the criteria to be included in *Chand's Top 50 Mutual Funds*.

Fidelity Canadian Asset Allocation Fund
Family: Fidelity Investments Canada
Tel: 800-263-4077
Web site: www.fidelity.ca

The Fidelity Canadian Asset Allocation Fund was launched in December 1994 and is managed by Richard Habermann, Alan Radlo, and Jeffrey Moore. Habermann, a CFA, is the lead manager and has been with the fund since its inception. Radlo, who has an MBA from the University of Massachusetts and is responsible for the equity portion of the fund, has also been with the fund since its inception. Moore, a CFA who has been with Fidelity since 1995, joined the fund last year and is responsible for its fixed income portion.

The objective of this fund is to provide a combination of long-term growth of capital, interest, and dividend income. To determine an acceptable asset mix, the managers consider a broad range of market and economic variables combined with analysis at the company level. As market conditions change, the managers alter asset-class weightings to maximize return while at the same time minimizing risk. Typically, the managers will make moderate changes to the asset mix, rather than sudden shifts. Individual securities are selected using a disciplined bottom-up approach to investing.

With close to $6.3 billion in assets, the fund is well-diversified and holds about 120 stocks and 150 bonds in its portfolio. About 50% of the portfolio is invested in Canadian equities, another 5% is in foreign equities, 35% is in bonds, and close to 10% is in cash. On the equity side, the fund's top holdings include Sun Life Financial, the National Bank of Canada, CP, Power Corporation, and the Bank of Montreal.

The Fidelity Canadian Asset Allocation Fund has an excellent risk/reward ranking and consistency record, and has beaten its peer group for 5 of the past 6 years. Although there is a 1-in-6 chance that returns will be negative over a 3-month period and a 1-in-17 chance they will be negative over a 1-year period, the fund has made money over all 3- and 5-year periods. Looking at all 5-year rolling periods, returns have averaged 15.8% and ranged from a high of 19.0% to a low of 13.0%.

Fund Facts

Fund:	FIDELITY CANADIAN ASSET ALLOCATION
Manager:	Richard Habermann, Alan Radlo, & Jeffrey Moore
Category:	Canadian Tactical Asset Allocation

Best/Worst Rolling Returns

3-Month Period

Best: 16.5%
Worst: -11.8%
Average: 3.7%
Times fund lost money: 18%

1-Year Period

Best: 41.6%
Worst: -3.0%
Average: 15.8%
Times fund lost money: 6%

3-Year Period

Best: 23.9%
Worst: 5.4%
Average: 15.1%
Times fund lost money: 0%

5-Year Period

Best: 19.0%
Worst: 13.0%
Average: 15.8%
Times fund lost money: 0%

Performance Record

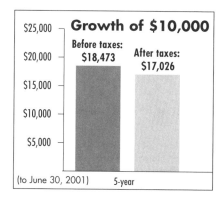

Growth of $10,000
Before taxes: $18,473
After taxes: $17,026
(to June 30, 2001) 5-year

Consistency Record 83%

Risk/Reward Ranking A

Tax-Efficiency Ratio 86%

Fund Details

Mgmt. Expense Ratio	2.49%	Sales charges	Yes
Minimum RRSP	$500	Minimum non-RRSP	$500

See chapter 13 for a discussion on how to interpret the Fund Facts page.

Mawer Canadian Diversified Investment Fund
Family: Mawer Mutual Funds
Tel: 888-549-6248
Web site: www.mawer.com

The Mawer Canadian Diversified Investment Fund was launched in January 1988 and has been managed by Donald Ferris since its inception. Ferris, a CFA with close to 25 years of investment experience, focusses on asset allocation strategies at Mawer Investment Management, a privately owned investment counselling firm based in Calgary.

The investment objective of this fund is to provide investors with a combination of long-term growth of capital and income. The fund invests in common and preferred shares and fixed income securities such as treasury bills, bonds, and debentures. In determining the optimal asset mix for the fund, Ferris uses a combination of quantitative and qualitative analysis. The fund follows a bottom-up growth investment strategy on the equity side with a large-cap bias, and also invests in other Mawer mutual funds.

With about $30 million in assets, the fund is well-diversified and holds close to 240 stocks and about 50 bonds in its portfolio. About 30% of the portfolio is invested in Canadian equities, with another 15% each in U.S. and international equities. Fixed income investments make up another 40% of the fund's assets. Investments in four other Mawer funds account for about 20% of the portfolio. Included in this group are Mawer's U.S. Equity Fund, World Investment Fund, New Canada Fund, and High Yield Bond Fund.

The Mawer Canadian Diversified Investment Fund has both a good risk/reward ranking and consistency record. The fund has beaten its peer group for 7 of the past 10 years. Although there is a 1-in-4 chance that returns will be negative over a 3-month period and a 1-in-9 chance they will be negative over a 1-year period, the fund has made money for its investors over all 3- and 5-year periods. Looking at all 5-year rolling periods, returns have averaged 10.7% and ranged from a high of 12.9% to a low of 8.1%.

Fund Facts

Fund: MAWER CANADIAN DIVERSIFIED INVESTMENT
Manager: Donald T. Ferris
Category: Canadian Tactical Asset Allocation

Best/Worst Rolling Returns

3-Month Period

Best: 11.2%
Worst: -11.6%
Average: 2.4%
Times fund lost money: 25%

1-Year Period

Best: 28.2%
Worst: -6.3%
Average: 10.0%
Times fund lost money: 11%

3-Year Period

Best: 16.6%
Worst: 4.1%
Average: 9.9%
Times fund lost money: 0%

5-Year Period

Best: 12.9%
Worst: 8.1%
Average: 10.7%
Times fund lost money: 0%

Performance Record

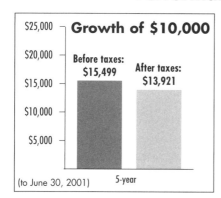

Growth of $10,000
Before taxes: $15,499
After taxes: $13,921
(to June 30, 2001) 5-year

Consistency Record 70%

Risk/Reward Ranking B

Tax-Efficiency Ratio 75%

Fund Details

Mgmt. Expense Ratio	1.31%	Sales charges	No
Minimum RRSP	$5,000	Minimum non-RRSP	$5,000

See chapter 13 for a discussion on how to interpret the Fund Facts page.

Chapter 28
Canadian Dividend Funds

Canadian dividend funds invest in dividend-paying preferred shares of corporations and in common shares that are expected to yield a high level of dividend income. These funds boast the added advantage that dividend income is taxed at a substantially lower rate than interest income. Canadian dividend funds are suitable for long-term investors who want income along with the potential for growth, and they are also a good choice for individuals who wish to maximize after-tax income by taking advantage of the dividend tax credit available. As a general rule, dividend funds are less volatile than other equity funds. These funds are unsuitable for investors with an investment time horizon of less than 5 years.

Of the close to 90 Canadian dividend funds, only six met the criteria to be included in the *Chand's Top 50 Mutual Funds*.

BMO Dividend Fund

Family: BMO Mutual Funds
Tel: 800-665-7700
Web site: www.bmo.com

The BMO Dividend Fund was launched in May 1994 and has been managed by Michael Stanley since October 1994. Stanley, the head of Canadian equity management at Jones Heward Investment Counsel, is a CFA with an MBA from the University of Toronto, and has 20 years of experience. Jones Heward, a subsidiary of the Bank of Montreal, is the advisor to the fund. Stanley is also the manager of the BMO Equity Fund, another top 50 Heavy Hitter fund.

The objective of this no-load fund is to provide investors with a high after-tax return, including dividend income and some capital-gains potential, by investing primarily in dividend-yielding common and preferred shares of established Canadian companies. Stanley focusses on the company's financial statistics, potential for growth, senior management, and quality of leadership. He also carefully monitors the companies that he invests in for any changes that may affect their profitability.

With close to $1.3 billion in assets, the fund follows a bottom-up/value investment strategy with a large-cap equity bias. The fund holds about 50 securities in its portfolio and has significant weightings in the financial services, utilities, pipelines, and oil and gas sectors, which together account for close to 90% of the portfolio. The fund's top 10 holdings include the Royal Bank of Canada, the Bank of Nova Scotia, Shell Canada, Imperial Oil, and Westcoast Energy.

The BMO Dividend Fund has an excellent risk/reward ranking and consistency record, having beaten its peer group for 5 of the past 6 years. During the 2000/2001 bear market, this fund posted a return of 13.6%, outperforming the average Canadian dividend fund, which posted a return of –5.7%. Although there is a 1-in-7 chance that returns will be negative over a 3-month period and a 1-in-14 chance they will be negative over a 1-year period, the fund has made money over all 3- and 5-year periods. Looking at all 5-year rolling periods, returns have averaged 18.7% and ranged from a high of 21.3% to a low of 15.8%.

Fund Facts

Fund:	BMO DIVIDEND
Manager:	Michael Stanley
Category:	Canadian Dividend

Best/Worst Rolling Returns

3-Month Period

Best: 19.8%
Worst: -22.1%
Average: 4.5%
Times fund lost money: 15%

1-Year Period

Best: 47.9%
Worst: -8.4%
Average: 20.0%
Times fund lost money: 7%

3-Year Period

Best: 30.0%
Worst: 8.7%
Average: 18.4%
Times fund lost money: 0%

5-Year Period

Best: 21.3%
Worst: 15.8%
Average: 18.7%
Times fund lost money: 0%

Performance Record

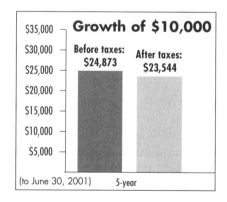

Growth of $10,000

Before taxes: $24,873
After taxes: $23,544

(to June 30, 2001)   5-year

Consistency Record	83%
Risk/Reward Ranking	A
Tax-Efficiency Ratio	94%

Fund Details

Mgmt. Expense Ratio	1.77%	Sales charges	No
Minimum RRSP	$500	Minimum non-RRSP	$500

See chapter 13 for a discussion on how to interpret the Fund Facts page.

HSBC Dividend Income Fund

Family: HSBC Investment Funds Canada
Tel: 800-830-8888
Web site: www.hsbc.ca

The HSBC Dividend Income Fund was launched in December 1994 and has been managed by the HSBC asset management investment team since its inception. The company emphasizes a team approach to fund management and capitalizes on the knowledge and expertise of its teams of investment professionals that are located in every major financial market around the world.

The investment objective of this no-load fund is to provide investors with dividend income combined with medium- to long-term growth of capital. The fund principally invests in high-yielding common and preferred shares of Canadian companies with a market capitalization of greater than $500 million, and is broadly diversified among industry sectors.

With close to $200 million in assets, the fund follows a top-down investment strategy with a large-cap equity bias. The fund holds about 65 stocks and a small number of bonds and has significant weightings in the financial services, utilities, pipelines, and oil and gas sectors. About 85% of the portfolio is invested in stocks, another 10% is in bonds, and the remainder is in cash. The fund's top 10 holdings make up just under 45% of the portfolio and include the Royal Bank of Canada, CIBC, BCE Inc., Power Financial Corporation, and Enbridge Inc.

The HSBC Dividend Income Fund has both a good risk/reward ranking and consistency record, having beaten its peer group for 5 of the past 6 years. During the 2000/2001 bear market, this fund posted a return of 1.1%, outperforming the average Canadian dividend fund, which posted a return of –5.7%. Although there is a 1-in-7 chance that returns will be negative over a 3-month period and a 1-in-10 chance they will be negative over a 1-year period, the fund has made money over all 3- and 5-year periods. Looking at all 5-year rolling periods, returns have averaged 15.7% and ranged from a high of 17.5% to a low of 13.9%.

Fund Facts

Fund:	HSBC DIVIDEND INCOME
Manager:	Management team
Category:	Canadian Dividend

Best/Worst Rolling Returns

3-Month Period

Best: 16.3%
Worst: -17.3%
Average: 3.6%
Times fund lost money: 13%

1-Year Period

Best: 36.4%
Worst: -4.9%
Average: 16.6%
Times fund lost money: 10%

3-Year Period

Best: 24.3%
Worst: 6.8%
Average: 14.3%
Times fund lost money: 0%

5-Year Period

Best: 17.5%
Worst: 13.9%
Average: 15.7%
Times fund lost money: 0%

Performance Record

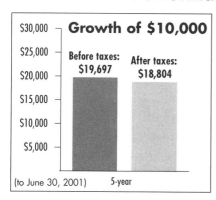

Growth of $10,000

Before taxes: $19,697
After taxes: $18,804

(to June 30, 2001)   5-year

Consistency Record 83%

Risk/Reward Ranking B

Tax-Efficiency Ratio 89%

Fund Details

Mgmt. Expense Ratio	2.01%	Sales charges	No
Minimum RRSP	$500	Minimum non-RRSP	$500

See chapter 13 for a discussion on how to interpret the Fund Facts page.

PH&N Dividend Income Fund
Family: Phillips, Hager & North Investment Management
Tel: 800-661-6141
Web site: www.phn.ca

The PH&N Dividend Income Fund was launched in June 1977 and is managed by the company's equity management team. Phillips, Hager & North, which emphasizes a team approach to investing, has been in business since 1964 and is one of Canada's largest investment firms. The company is well known for its investment philosophy that combines a disciplined approach with a commitment to minimizing risk.

The investment objective of this no-load fund is to provide investors with dividend income combined with long-term growth of capital, by investing primarily in the common and preferred shares of well-established Canadian companies. With over $1.1 billion in assets, the fund follows a bottom-up investment strategy that is a blend of growth and value and has a large-cap equity bias.

The fund holds about 40 stocks in its portfolio and has significant weightings in the financial services, industrial products, utilities, and pipelines sectors, which together account for over 70% of the portfolio. The fund's top 10 holdings make up just over 50% of the portfolio and include the Royal Bank of Canada, CIBC, Manulife Financial Corporation, Magna International, Suncor Energy, and Enbridge Inc.

The PH&N Dividend Income Fund has both an excellent risk/reward ranking and consistency record, having beaten its peer group for 9 of the past 10 years. During the 2000/2001 bear market, the fund posted a return of 11.7%, outperforming the average Canadian dividend fund, which posted a return of –5.7%. Although there is a 1-in-5 chance that returns will be negative over a 3-month period and a 1-in-10 chance they will be negative over a 1-year period, the fund has made money for its investors over all 3- and 5-year periods. Looking at all 5-year rolling periods, returns have averaged 19.9% and ranged from a high of 25.7% to a low of 11.0%. The fund, with a tax-efficiency ratio of 100% over 5 years, is also an excellent choice for investors seeking a tax-efficient dividend fund for their non-registered accounts.

Fund Facts

Fund:	PH&N DIVIDEND INCOME
Manager:	Management team
Category:	Canadian Dividend

Best/Worst Rolling Returns

3-Month Period

Best: 21.5%
Worst: -21.6%
Average: 4.3%
Times fund lost money: 21%

1-Year Period

Best: 57.9%
Worst: -6.9%
Average: 19.2%
Times fund lost money: 10%

3-Year Period

Best: 33.0%
Worst: 7.6%
Average: 18.1%
Times fund lost money: 0%

5-Year Period

Best: 25.7%
Worst: 11.0%
Average: 19.9%
Times fund lost money: 0%

Performance Record

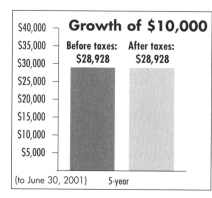

Growth of $10,000
Before taxes: $28,928
After taxes: $28,928
(to June 30, 2001) 5-year

Consistency Record 90%

Risk/Reward Ranking A

Tax-Efficiency Ratio 100%

Fund Details

Mgmt. Expense Ratio	1.21%	Sales charges	No
Minimum RRSP	$25,000	Minimum non-RRSP	$25,000

See chapter 13 for a discussion on how to interpret the Fund Facts page.

Royal Dividend Fund

Family: Royal Mutual Funds
Tel: 800-463-3863
Web site: www.royalbank.com

The Royal Dividend Fund was launched in January 1993 and has been managed by John Kellett since its inception. Kellett, a graduate of McGill University and a CFA, has over 30 years of investment experience. He is a vice-president with Royal Bank Investment Management Inc. and a member of the bank's Canadian equity and stock selection committee and investment policy committee.

The investment objective of this no-load fund is to provide investors with long-term total returns consisting of regular dividend income payments and modest long-term capital growth. The fund invests primarily in Canadian companies with above-average dividend yields. With close to $2.2 billion in assets, the fund follows a bottom-up/value investment strategy with a large-cap equity bias.

The fund holds about 40 stocks in its portfolio and has significant weightings in the financial services, utilities, pipelines, and oil and gas sectors, which together account for over 70% of the portfolio. The fund's top 10 holdings make up over 55% of the portfolio and include CIBC, the Bank of Nova Scotia, TransCanada PipeLines, Enbridge Inc., and Westcoast Energy.

The Royal Dividend Fund has an excellent risk/reward ranking and a solid consistency record, having beaten its peer group for 6 of the past 7 years. During the 2000/2001 bear market, the fund posted a return of 10.1%, outperforming the average Canadian dividend fund, which posted a return of –5.7%. Although there is a 1-in-6 chance that returns will be negative over a 3-month period and a 1-in-8 chance they will be negative over a 1-year period, the fund has made money for its investors over all 3- and 5-year periods. Looking at all 5-year rolling periods, returns have averaged 17.4% and ranged from a high of 21.1% to a low of 14.1%.

Fund Facts

Fund:	ROYAL DIVIDEND
Manager:	John Kellett
Category:	Canadian Dividend

Best/Worst Rolling Returns

3-Month Period

Best: 22.3%
Worst: -20.3%
Average: 3.8%
Times fund lost money: 17%

1-Year Period

Best: 51.3%
Worst: -7.1%
Average: 16.1%
Times fund lost money: 12%

3-Year Period

Best: 29.9%
Worst: 6.0%
Average: 16.5%
Times fund lost money: 0%

5-Year Period

Best: 21.1%
Worst: 14.1%
Average: 17.4%
Times fund lost money: 0%

Performance Record

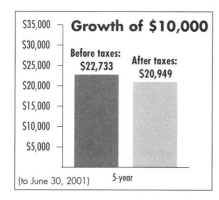

Growth of $10,000
Before taxes: $22,733
After taxes: $20,949
(to June 30, 2001) 5-year

Consistency Record 86%

Risk/Reward Ranking A

Tax-Efficiency Ratio 89%

Fund Details

Mgmt. Expense Ratio	1.88%	Sales charges	No
Minimum RRSP	$500	Minimum non-RRSP	$1,000

See chapter 13 for a discussion on how to interpret the Fund Facts page.

Scotia Canadian Dividend Fund
Family: Scotia Mutual Funds
Tel: 800-268-9269
Web site: www.scotiabank.com

The Scotia Canadian Dividend Fund was launched in October 1992. Scotiabank emphasizes a team approach in the management of their mutual funds and the Scotia Canadian Dividend Fund is managed by the Scotia Cassels investment management team, the advisors to the fund.

The investment objective of this no-load fund is to provide investors with a high level of dividend income combined with the potential for long-term capital growth. It invests primarily in dividend-paying common and preferred shares of well-established Canadian companies. With over $910 million in assets, the fund follows a top-down investment strategy that is a blend of growth and value and has a large-cap equity bias.

The fund holds about 70 stocks in its portfolio and has significant weightings in the financial services, utilities, and oil and gas sectors, which together account for about 65% of the portfolio. The fund's top 10 holdings make up over 40% of the portfolio and include BCE Inc., CIBC, the Bank of Montreal, BC Gas, TransCanada PipeLines, and Manitoba Telecom Services Inc.

The Scotia Canadian Dividend Fund has an excellent risk/reward ranking and a solid consistency record, having beaten its peer group for 6 of the past 8 years. During the 2000/2001 bear market, the fund posted a return of 6.8%, outperforming the average Canadian dividend fund, which posted a return of –5.7%. Although there is a 1-in-5 chance that returns will be negative over a 3-month period and a 1-in-7 chance they will be negative over a 1-year period, the fund has made money for its investors over all 3- and 5-year periods. Looking at all 5-year rolling periods, returns have averaged 16.1% and ranged from a high of 19.2% to a low of 12.5%. The fund also has a very good tax-efficiency ratio of 92% over a 5-year period.

Fund Facts

Fund:	SCOTIA CANADIAN DIVIDEND
Manager:	Management team
Category:	Canadian Dividend

Best/Worst Rolling Returns

3-Month Period

Best: 17.2%
Worst: -18.7%
Average: 3.5%
Times fund lost money: 22%

1-Year Period

Best: 49.9%
Worst: -9.2%
Average: 14.9%
Times fund lost money: 14%

3-Year Period

Best: 27.8%
Worst: 6.4%
Average: 15.0%
Times fund lost money: 0%

5-Year Period

Best: 19.2%
Worst: 12.5%
Average: 16.1%
Times fund lost money: 0%

Performance Record

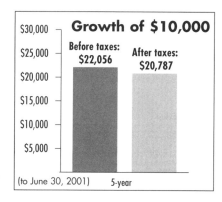

Growth of $10,000
Before taxes: $22,056
After taxes: $20,787
(to June 30, 2001) 5-year

Consistency Record 75%

Risk/Reward Ranking A

Tax-Efficiency Ratio 92%

Fund Details

Mgmt. Expense Ratio	1.14%	Sales charges	No
Minimum RRSP	$500	Minimum non-RRSP	$500

See chapter 13 for a discussion on how to interpret the Fund Facts page.

Standard Life Canadian Dividend Fund

Family: Standard Life Mutual Funds
Tel: 800-665-6237
Web site: www.standardlife.ca

The Standard Life Canadian Dividend Fund was launched in November 1994 and is managed by the firm's investment management team. Standard Life emphasizes a team approach in the management of their mutual funds. Fundamental internal research is the cornerstone of the company's investment philosophy and the company generates 75% of their research through proprietary models.

The investment objective of this load fund is to provide investors with a high level of dividend income combined with the potential for long-term capital growth. It invests in a diversified portfolio of primarily high-quality and high-yielding common stocks of Canadian companies. With over $165 million in assets, the fund follows a bottom-up investment strategy that is a blend of growth and value and has a large-cap equity bias.

The fund holds about 40 stocks in its portfolio and is heavily concentrated in the financial services sector, which accounts for over 40% of the portfolio. It also has around 10% each in the oil and gas and communications sectors. The fund's top 10 holdings make up close to 45% of the portfolio and include the Bank of Nova Scotia, CIBC, Toronto-Dominion Bank, the Bank of Montreal, Imperial Oil, and PanCanadian Petroleum.

The Standard Life Canadian Dividend Fund has both an excellent risk/reward ranking and consistency record, having beaten its peer group for each of the past 6 years. During the 2000/2001 bear market, the fund posted a return of 11.0%, outperforming the average Canadian dividend fund, which posted a return of –5.7%. Although there is a 1-in-8 chance that returns will be negative over a 3-month period and a 1-in-10 chance they will be negative over a 1-year period, the fund has made money for its investors over all 3- and 5-year periods. Looking at all 5-year rolling periods, returns have averaged 21.4% and ranged from a high of 23.5% to a low of 19.1%. The fund also has a very good tax-efficiency ratio of 92% over a 5-year period.

Fund Facts

Fund:	STANDARD LIFE CANADIAN DIVIDEND
Manager:	Management team
Category:	Canadian Dividend

Best/Worst Rolling Returns

3-Month Period

Best: 21.5%
Worst: -26.1%
Average: 5.1%
Times fund lost money: 12%

1-Year Period

Best: 54.2%
Worst: -9.2%
Average: 22.7%
Times fund lost money: 10%

3-Year Period

Best: 34.7%
Worst: 8.1%
Average: 20.5%
Times fund lost money: 0%

5-Year Period

Best: 23.5%
Worst: 19.1%
Average: 21.4%
Times fund lost money: 0%

Performance Record

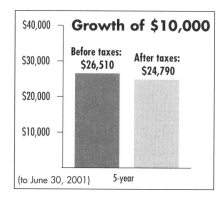

Growth of $10,000
Before taxes: $26,510
After taxes: $24,790
(to June 30, 2001) 5-year

Consistency Record   100%

Risk/Reward Ranking   A

Tax-Efficiency Ratio   92%

Fund Details

Mgmt. Expense Ratio	1.50%	Sales charges	Yes
Minimum RRSP	$1,000	Minimum non-RRSP	$1,000

See chapter 13 for a discussion on how to interpret the Fund Facts page.

Chapter 29
Global Balanced and Asset Allocation Funds

Global balanced and asset allocation funds invest in a diversified portfolio of securities, including stocks, bonds, and cash and cash equivalents, with at least 25% of these securities in non-Canadian investments. These funds have no restrictions on asset weightings and can allocate assets depending upon various factors, such as market outlook and conditions. The goal of this type of fund is to provide investors with long-term capital growth—through increases in stock prices—as well as income. Because of the foreign content, these funds will be influenced by exchange-rate fluctuations. Global balanced and asset allocation funds are suitable for investors who seek long-term capital growth as well as additional income and have an investment time horizon of at least 5 years. These funds are also suitable for investors who seek further diversification. They are unsuitable for investors with short investment time horizons or those who are uncomfortable with the risks inherent in investing in overseas markets.

Of the close to 250 global balanced and asset allocation funds, only one met the criteria to be included in *Chand's Top 50 Mutual Funds*.

CI International Balanced Fund

Family: CI Mutual Funds
Tel: 800-563-5181
Web site: www.cifunds.com

The CI International Balanced Fund was launched in October 1994 and has been managed by William Sterling since its inception. Sterling has a PhD from Harvard University and is a chief investment officer with CI Global Advisors. With over 18 years of investment experience, he is the co-author of the best-selling book Boomernomics which focussed on how to integrate demographics and investing. Sterling is also the manager of the CI Global Fund, another top 50 Heavy Hitter fund.

The investment objective of this load fund is to provide investors with a high level of total return. To achieve this objective, the fund invests in stocks and fixed income securities of issuers located throughout the world. In selecting securities for the portfolio, Sterling is not limited to how much he invests in a country or asset class but varies the asset mix depending on market conditions.

With over $1.8 billion in assets, about 55% of the fund's assets are invested in stocks, about 25% is in bonds, and the remainder is in cash. Geographically, about 40% of the fund's holdings are invested in the United States, 20% is invested in Canada, and about 7% each is in Japan and Europe. On the equity side, the fund has significant weightings in consumer products, financial services, industrial products, and communications and media. The fund's top 10 equity holdings include Citigroup Inc., General Electric, AT&T, Alcoa Inc., and the Walt Disney Company.

The CI International Balanced Fund has both an excellent risk/reward ranking and consistency record, having beaten its peer group for each of the past 6 years. Although there is a 1-in-4 chance that returns will be negative over a 3-month period and a 1-in-14 chance they will be negative over a 1-year period, the fund has made money for its investors over all 3- and 5-year periods. Looking at all 5-year rolling periods, returns have averaged 14.3% and ranged from a high of 18.0% to a low of 9.1%.

Fund Facts

Fund:	CI INTERNATIONAL BALANCED
Manager:	William Sterling
Category:	Global Balanced and Asset Allocation

Best/Worst Rolling Returns

3-Month Period

Best: 19.0%
Worst: -11.6%
Average: 2.8%
Times fund lost money: 27%

1-Year Period

Best: 29.8%
Worst: -16.1%
Average: 13.7%
Times fund lost money: 7%

3-Year Period

Best: 20.1%
Worst: 3.4%
Average: 14.6%
Times fund lost money: 0%

5-Year Period

Best: 18.0%
Worst: 9.1%
Average: 14.3%
Times fund lost money: 0%

Performance Record

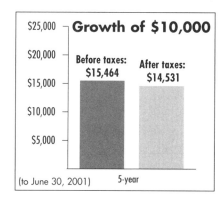

Growth of $10,000

Before taxes: $15,464
After taxes: $14,531

(to June 30, 2001)　5-year

Consistency Record	100%
Risk/Reward Ranking	A
Tax-Efficiency Ratio	85%

Fund Details

Mgmt. Expense Ratio	2.50%	Sales charges	Yes
Minimum RRSP	$500	Minimum non-RRSP	$500

See chapter 13 for a discussion on how to interpret the Fund Facts page.

About the Author

Ranga Chand is recognized both domestically and internationally as one of Canada's leading economists and mutual fund analysts. Professionally, he held senior positions with Canada's Department of Finance, then served as a director of the Conference Board of Canada, before joining a major stockbrokerage firm. He has also taught economics at the University of Waterloo, published extensively in the field of economics, and represented Canada at numerous economic forums, including the OECD in Paris, the United Nations, and the World Institute of Economics in Germany.

Much in demand by organizations, industries, and associations throughout North America, Ranga Chand is well known for his down-to-earth, clear, and informative presentations on the subjects of the global economy and investing. He can be seen every Monday at 3:00pm and 8:30pm ET on ROBTV's popular show "Talking Mutual Funds with Ranga Chand" and is interviewed regularly by radio and the national print media. He is also the author of the annual U.S. guide, *Best of the Best Mutual Funds*, featuring America's top 50 Heavy Hitter funds, and *Ranga Chand's Getting Started in Mutual Funds*.

Ranga Chand is founder and president of the research firm Chand Carmichael & Company Limited, located in Oakville, Ontario.

Ranga Chand is always interested in hearing from his readers and may be reached by writing to: Ranga Chand, Chand Carmichael & Company Limited, Suite 622, 2689 Lakeshore Road East, Oakville, Ontario, L6J 7S4.

If you would like information on Ranga Chand's customized seminars and workshops for corporations and associations, please telephone (905) 844-6708 or e-mail rangachand@sympatico.ca.